THE CHRISTIAN YEAR

BY

JOHN KEBLE

THE CHRISTIAN YEAR

Thoughts in Verse
For The
Sundays and Holidays
Throughout The Year

BY THE
REV. JOHN KEBLE

In quietness and in confidence shall be
your strength.

ISAIAH XXX.15

ADVERTISEMENT

Next to a sound rule of faith, there is nothing of so much consequence as a sober standard of feeling in matters of practical religion; and it is the peculiar happiness of the Church of England to possess, in her authorized formularies, an ample and secure provision for both. But in times of much leisure and unbounded curiosity, when excitement of every kind is sought after with a morbid eagerness, this part of the merit of our Liturgy, is likely in some measure to be lost, on many even of its sincere admirers: the very tempers which most require such discipline, setting themselves, in general, most decidedly against it. The object of the present publication will be attained, if any person find assistance from it in bringing his own thoughts and feelings into more entire unison with those recommended and exemplified in the Prayer Book. The work does not furnish a complete series of compositions; being, in many parts, rather adapted with more or less propriety to the successive portions of the Liturgy, than originally suggested by them. Something has been added at the end concerning the several Occasional Services: which constitute, from their personal and domestic nature, the most perfect instance of that soothing tendency in the Prayer Book, which it is the chief purpose of these pages to exhibit.

MAY 30th, 1827

Contents

MORNING

His compassions fail not. They are new every morning. Lament.
iii. 22, 23.

Hues of the rich unfolding morn,
That, ere the glorious sun be born,

By some soft touch invisible
Around his path are taught to swell; -

Thou rustling breeze so fresh and gay,
That dancest forth at opening day,
And brushing by with joyous wing,
Wakenest each little leaf to sing; -

Ye fragrant clouds of dewy steam,
By which deep grove and tangled stream
Pay, for soft rains in season given,
Their tribute to the genial heaven; -

Why waste your treasures of delight
Upon our thankless, joyless sight;
Who day by day to sin awake,
Seldom of Heaven and you partake?

Oh! timely happy, timely wise,
Hearts that with rising morn arise!
Eyes that the beam celestial view,
Which evermore makes all things new! [1]

New every morning is the love
Our wakening and uprising prove;
Through sleep and darkness safely brought,
Restored to life, and power, and thought.

New mercies, each returning day,
Hover around us while we pray;
New perils past, new sins forgiven,
New thoughts of God, new hopes of Heaven.

If on our daily course our mind
Be set to hallow all we find,
New treasures still, of countless price,
God will provide for sacrifice.

Old friends, old scenes will lovelier be,
As more of Heaven in each we see:
Some softening gleam of love and prayer
Shall dawn on every cross and care.

As for some dear familiar strain
Untir'd we ask, and ask again,
Ever, in its melodious store,
Finding a spell unheard before;

Such is the bliss of souls serene,
When they have sworn, and stedfast mean,
Counting the cost, in all t' espy
Their God, in all themselves deny.

Oh, could we learn that sacrifice,
What lights would all around us rise!
How would our hearts with wisdom talk
Along Life's dullest, dreariest walk!

We need not bid, for cloister'd cell,
Our neighbour and our work farewell,

Nor strive to wind ourselves too high
For sinful man beneath the sky:

The trivial round, the common task,
Would furnish all we ought to ask;
Room to deny ourselves; a road
To bring us daily nearer God.

Seek we no more; content with these,
Let present Rapture, Comfort, Ease,
As Heaven shall bid them, come and go: -
The secret this of Rest below.

Only, O Lord, in Thy dear love
Fit us for perfect Rest above;
And help us, this and every day,
To live more nearly as we pray.

[1] Revelation xxi. 5.

EVENING

Abide with us: for it is toward evening, and the day is far spent. -
St.Luke xxiv. 29.

'Tis gone, that bright and orbed blaze,
Fast fading from our wistful gaze;
You mantling cloud has hid from sight
The last faint pulse of quivering light.

In darkness and in weariness
The traveller on his way must press,
No gleam to watch on tree or tower,
Whiling away the lonesome hour.

Sun of my soul! Thou Saviour dear,
It is not night if Thou be near:
Oh, may no earth-born cloud arise
To hide Thee from Thy servant's eyes!

When round Thy wondrous works below
My searching rapturous glance I throw,
Tracing out Wisdom, Power and Love,
In earth or sky, in stream or grove; -

Or by the light Thy words disclose
Watch Time's full river as it flows,
Scanning Thy gracious Providence,
Where not too deep for mortal sense: -

When with dear friends sweet talk I hold,
And all the flowers of life unfold;
Let not my heart within me burn,
Except in all I Thee discern.
When the soft dews of kindly sleep
My wearied eyelids gently steep,
Be my last thought, how sweet to rest
For ever on my Saviour's breast.

Abide with me from morn till eve,
For without Thee I cannot live:
Abide with me when night is nigh,
For without Thee I dare not die.

Thou Framer of the light and dark,
Steer through the tempest Thine own ark:
Amid the howling wintry sea
We are in port if we have Thee. [2]

The Rulers of this Christian land,
'Twixt Thee and us ordained to stand, -
Guide Thou their course, O Lord, aright,
Let all do all as in Thy sight.

Oh! by Thine own sad burthen, borne
So meekly up the hill of scorn,
Teach Thou Thy Priests their daily cross
To bear as Thine, nor count it loss!

If some poor wandering child of Thine
Have spurn'd to-day the voice divine,
Now, Lord, the gracious work begin;
Let him no more lie down in sin.

Watch by the sick: enrich the poor
With blessings from Thy boundless store:

Be every mourner's sleep to-night,
Like infant's slumbers, pure and light.

Come near and bless us when we wake,
Ere through the world our way we take;
Till in the ocean of Thy love
We lose ourselves, in Heaven above.

[2] Then they willingly received Him into the ship: and immediately the ship was at the land whither they went. St. John vi. 21.

ADVENT SUNDAY

Now it is high time to awake out of sleep: for now is our salva-
tion nearer than when we believed. - Romans xiii 11.

Awake - again the Gospel-trump is blown -
From year to year it swells with louder tone,
From year to year the signs of wrath
Are gathering round the Judge's path,
Strange words fulfill'd, and mighty works achiev'd,
And truth in all the world both hated and believ'd.

Awake! why linger in the gorgeous town,
Sworn liegemen of the Cross and thorny crown?
Up from your beds of sloth for shame,
Speed to the eastern mount like flame,

Nor wonder, should ye find your King in tears,
E'en with the loud Hosanna ringing in His ears.
Alas! no need to rouse them: long ago
They are gone forth to swell Messiah's show:
With glittering robes and garlands sweet
They strew the ground beneath His feet:
All but your hearts are there - O doom'd to prove
The arrows wing'd in Heaven for Faith that will not love!

Meanwhile He passes through th' adoring crowd,
Calm as the march of some majestic cloud,
That o'er wild scenes of ocean-war

Holds its still course in Heaven afar:
E'en so, heart-searching Lord, as years roll on,
Thou keepest silent watch from Thy triumphal throne:

E'en so, the world is thronging round to gaze
On the dread vision of the latter days,
Constrain'd to own Thee, but in heart
Prepar'd to take Barabbas' part:
"Hosanna" now, to-morrow "Crucify,"
The changeful burden still of their rude lawless cry.

Yet in that throng of selfish hearts untrue
Thy sad eye rests upon Thy faithful few,
Children and childlike souls are there,
Blind Bartimeus' humble prayer,
And Lazarus waken'd from his four days' sleep,
Enduring life again, that Passover to keep.

And fast beside the olive-border'd way
Stands the bless'd home where Jesus deign'd to stay,
The peaceful home, to Zeal sincere
And heavenly Contemplation dear,
Where Martha lov'd to wait with reverence meet,
And wiser Mary linger'd at Thy sacred feet.

Still through decaying ages as they glide,
Thou lov'st Thy chosen remnant to divide;
Sprinkled along the waste of years
Full many a soft green isle appears:
Pause where we may upon the desert road,
Some shelter is in sight, some sacred safe abode.

When withering blasts of error swept the sky, [3]
And Love's last flower seem'd fain to droop and die,
How sweet, how lone the ray benign
On shelter'd nooks of Palestine!
Then to his early home did Love repair, [4]

And cheer'd his sickening heart with his own native air.

Years roll away: again the tide of crime
Has swept Thy footsteps from the favour'd clime
Where shall the holy Cross find rest?
On a crowned monarch's [5] mailed breast:
Like some bright angel o'er the darkling scene,
Through court and camp he holds his heavenward course serene.

A fouler vision yet; an age of light,
Light without love, glares on the aching sight:
Oh, who can tell how calm and sweet,
Meek Walton, shows thy green retreat,
When wearied with the tale thy times disclose,
The eye first finds thee out in thy secure repose?

Thus bad and good their several warnings give
Of His approach, whom none may see and live:
Faith's ear, with awful still delight,
Counts them like minute-bells at night.
Keeping the heart awake till dawn of morn,
While to her funeral pile this aged world is borne.

But what are Heaven's alarms to hearts that cower
In wilful slumber, deepening every hour,
That draw their curtains closer round,
The nearer swells the trumpet's sound?
Lord, ere our trembling lamps sink down and die,
Touch us with chastening hand, and make us feel Thee nigh.

[3] Arianism in the fourth century.
[4] See St. Jerome's Works, i. 123, edit. Erasm.
[5] St. Louis in the thirteenth century.

SECOND SUNDAY IN ADVENT

And when these things begin to pass, then look up, and lift up your heads; for your redemption draweth night. St. Luke xxi. 28.

Not till the freezing blast is still,
Till freely leaps the sparkling rill,
And gales sweep soft from summer skies,
As o'er a sleeping infant's eyes
A mother's kiss; ere calls like these,
No sunny gleam awakes the trees,
Nor dare the tender flowerets show
Their bosoms to th' uncertain glow.

Why then, in sad and wintry time,
Her heavens all dark with doubt and crime,
Why lifts the Church her drooping head,
As though her evil hour were fled?
Is she less wise than leaves of spring,
Or birds that cower with folded wing?
What sees she in this lowering sky
To tempt her meditative eye?

She has a charm, a word of fire,
A pledge of love that cannot tire;
By tempests, earthquakes, and by wars,
By rushing waves and falling stars,
By every sign her Lord foretold,
She sees the world is waxing old, [6]
And through that last and direst storm

Descries by faith her Saviour's form.

Not surer does each tender gem,
Set in the fig-tree's polish'd stem,
Foreshow the summer season bland,
Than these dread signs Thy mighty hand:
But, oh, frail hearts, and spirits dark!
The season's flight unwarn'd we mark,
But miss the Judge behind the door, [7]
For all the light of sacred lore:

Yet is He there; beneath our eaves
Each sound His wakeful ear receives:
Hush, idle words, and thoughts of ill,
Your Lord is listening: peace, be still. [8]
Christ watches by a Christian's hearth,
Be silent, 'vain deluding mirth,.'
Till in thine alter'd voice be known
Somewhat of Resignation's tone.

But chiefly ye should lift your gaze
Above the world's uncertain haze,
And look with calm unwavering eye
On the bright fields beyond the sky,
Ye, who your Lord's commission bear
His way of mercy to prepare:
Angels He calls ye: be your strife
To lead on earth an Angel's life.

Think not of rest; though dreams be sweet,
Start up, and ply your heavenward feet.
Is not God's oath upon your head,
Ne'er to sink back on slothful bed,
Never again your loans untie,
Nor let your torches waste and die,
Till, when the shadows thickest fall,
Ye hear your Master's midnight call?

[6] The world hath lost its youth, and the times begin to wax old.
2 Esdras xiv. 10.
[7] See St. James v. 9.
[8] Iba fabulantur, ut qui sciant Dominum audire, Tertull. Apolog.
p. 36 edit. Higalz.

THIRD SUNDAY IN ADVENT

What went ye out into the wilderness to see? A reed shaken with the wind? . . . But what went ye out for to see? A prophet? yea, I say unto you, and more than a prophet. St. Matthew xi. 7, 9.

What went ye out to see
O'er the rude sandy lea,
Where stately Jordan flows by many a palm,
Or where Gennesaret's wave
Delights the flowers to lave,
That o'er her western slope breathe airs of balm?

All through the summer night,
Those blossoms red and bright [9]
Spread their soft breasts, unheeding, to the breeze,
Like hermits watching still
Around the sacred hill,
Where erst our Saviour watched upon His knees.

The Paschal moon above
Seems like a saint to rove,
Left shining in the world with Christ alone;
Below, the lake's still face
Sleeps sweetly in th' embrace
Of mountains terrac'd high with mossy stone.

Here may we sit, and dream
Over the heavenly theme,

Till to our soul the former days return;
Till on the grassy bed,
Where thousands once He fed,
The world's incarnate Maker we discern.

O cross no more the main,
Wandering so will and vain,
To count the reeds that tremble in the wind,
On listless dalliance bound,
Like children gazing round,
Who on God's works no seal of Godhead find.

Bask not in courtly bower,
Or sun-bright hall of power,
Pass Babel quick, and seek the holy land '
From robes of Tyrian dye
Turn with undazzled eye
To Bethlehem's glade, or Carmel's haunted strand.

Or choose thee out a cell
In Kedron's storied dell,
Beside the springs of Love, that never die;
Among the olives kneel
The chill night-blast to feel,
And watch the Moon that saw thy Master's agony.

Then rise at dawn of day,
And wind thy thoughtful way,
Where rested once the Temple's stately shade,
With due feet tracing round
The city's northern bound,
To th' other holy garden, where the Lord was laid.

Who thus alternate see
His death and victory,
Rising and falling as on angel wings,
They, while they seem to roam,

Draw daily nearer home,
Their heart untravell'd still adores the King of kings.

Or, if at home they stay,
Yet are they, day by day,
In spirit journeying through the glorious land,
Not for light Fancy's reed,
Nor Honour's purple meed,
Nor gifted Prophet's lore, nor Science' wondrous wand.

But more than Prophet, more
Than Angels can adore
With face unveil'd, is He they go to seek:
Blessed be God, Whose grace
Shows Him in every place
To homeliest hearts of pilgrims pure and meek.

[9] Rhododendrons: with which the western bank of the lake is said to be clothed down to the water's edge.

FOURTH SUNDAY IN ADVENT

The eyes of them that see shall not be dim, and the ears of them
that hear shall hearken. Isaiah xxxii. 3.

Of the bright things in earth and air
How little can the heart embrace!
Soft shades and gleaming lights are there '
I know it well, but cannot trace.

Mine eye unworthy seems to read
One page of Nature's beauteous book;
It lies before me, fair outspread '
I only cast a wishful look.

I cannot paint to Memory's eye
The scene, the glance, I dearest love '
Unchang'd themselves, in me they die,
Or faint or false their shadows prove.

In vain, with dull and tuneless ear,
I linger by soft Music's cell,
And in my heart of hearts would hear
What to her own she deigns to tell.

'Tis misty all, both sight and sound '
I only know 'tis fair and sweet '
'Tis wandering on enchanted ground

With dizzy brow and tottering feet.

But patience! there may come a time
When these dull ears shall scan aright
Strains that outring Earth's drowsy chime,
As Heaven outshines the taper's light.

These eyes, that dazzled now and weak,
At glancing motes in sunshine wink.
Shall see the King's [10] full glory break,
Nor from the blissful vision shrink:

In fearless love and hope uncloy'd
For ever on that ocean bright
Empower'd to gaze; and undestroy'd,
Deeper and deeper plunge in light.

Though scarcely now their laggard glance
Reach to an arrow's flight, that day
They shall behold, and not in trance,
The region 'very far away.'

If Memory sometimes at our spell
Refuse to speak, or speak amiss,
We shall not need her where we dwell
Ever in sight of all our bliss.

Meanwhile, if over sea or sky
Some tender lights unnotic'd fleet,
Or on lov'd features dawn and die,
Unread, to us, their lesson sweet;

Yet are there saddening sights around,
Which Heaven, in mercy, spares us too,
And we see far in holy ground,
If duly purg'd our mental view.

The distant landscape draws not nigh
For all our gazing; but the soul,
That upward looks, may still descry
Nearer, each day, the brightening goal.

And thou, too curious ear, that fain
Wouldst thread the maze of Harmony,
Content thee with one simple strain,
The lowlier, sure, the worthier thee;

Till thou art duly train'd, and taught
The concord sweet of Love divine:
Then, with that inward Music fraught,
For ever rise, and sing, and shine.

[10] Thine eyes shall see the King in His beauty: they shall behold the landthat is very far off. Isaiah xxxiii. 17.

CHRISTMAS DAY

And suddenly there was with the Angel a multitude of the heav-
enly host, praising God. St. Luke ii. 13.

What sudden blaze of song
Spreads o'er th' expanse of Heav'n?
In waves of light it thrills along,
Th' angelic signal given '
'Glory to God!' from yonder central fire
Flows out the echoing lay beyond the starry choir;

Like circles widening round
Upon a clear blue river,
Orb after orb, the wondrous sound
Is echoed on for ever:
'Glory to God on high, on earth be peace,
And love towards men of love [11] - salvation and release.'

Yet stay, before thou dare
To join that festal throng;
Listen and mark what gentle air
First stirr'd the tide of song;
'Tis not, 'the Saviour born in David's home,
To Whom for power and health obedient worlds 'should come:'
'

'Tis not, 'the Christ the Lord:'
With fix'd adoring look

The choir of Angels caught the word,
Nor yet their silence broke:
But when they heard the sign where Christ should be,
In sudden light they shone and heavenly harmony.

Wrapp'd in His swaddling bands,
And in His manger laid,
The Hope and Glory of all lands
Is come to the world's aid:
No peaceful home upon his cradle smil'd,
Guests rudely went and came, where slept the royal Child.

But where Thou dwellest, Lord,
No other thought should be,
Once duly welcom'd and ador'd,
How should I part with Thee?
Bethlehem must lose Thee soon, but Thou wilt grace
The single heart to be Thy sure abiding-place.

Thee, on the bosom laid
Of a pure virgin mind,
In quiet ever, and in shade,
Shepherd and sage may find;
They, who have bowed untaught to Nature's sway,
And they, who follow Truth along her star-pav'd way.

The pastoral spirits first
Approach Thee, Babe divine,
For they in lowly thoughts are nurs'd,
Meet for Thy lowly shrine:
Sooner than they should miss where Thou dost dwell,
Angels from Heaven will stoop to guide them to Thy cell.

Still, as the day comes round
For Thee to be reveal'd,
By wakeful shepherds Thou art found,
Abiding in the field.

All through the wintry heaven and chill night air,
In music and in light Thou dawnest on their prayer.

O faint not ye for fear '
What though your wandering sheep,
Reckless of what they see and hear,
Lie lost in wilful sleep?
High Heaven in mercy to your sad annoy
Still greets you with glad tidings of immortal joy.

Think on th' eternal home,
The Saviour left for you;
Think on the Lord most holy, come
To dwell with hearts untrue:
So shall ye tread untir'd His pastoral ways,
And in the darkness sing your carol of high praise.

[11] I have ventured to adopt the reading of the Vulgate, as being generally known through Pergolesi's beautiful composition, 'Gloria in excelsis Deo, et in terra pax hominibus bon¦ voluntatis.'

ST. STEPHEN'S DAY

He, being full of the Holy Ghost, looked up steadfastly into
heaven, and saw the glory of God, and Jesus standing on the
right hand of God.
Acts vii. 55.

As rays around the source of light
Stream upward ere he glow in sight,
And watching by his future flight
Set the clear heavens on fire;
So on the King of Martyrs wait
Three chosen bands, in royal state, [12]
And all earth owns, of good and great,
Is gather'd in that choir.

One presses on, and welcomes death:
One calmly yields his willing breath,
Nor slow, nor hurrying, but in faith
Content to die or live:

And some, the darlings of their Lord,
Play smiling with the flame and sword,
And, ere they speak, to His sure word
Unconscious witness give.
Foremost and nearest to His throne,
By perfect robes of triumph known,
And likest Him in look and tone,

The holy Stephen kneels,
With stedfast gaze, as when the sky
Flew open to his fainting eye,
Which, like a fading lamp, flash'd high,
Seeing what death conceals.

Well might you guess what vision bright
Was present to his raptur'd sight,
E'en as reflected streams of light
Their solar source betray '
The glory which our God surrounds,
The Son of Man, th' atoning wounds '
He sees them all; and earth's dull bounds
Are melting fast away.

He sees them all - no other view
Could stamp the Saviour's likeness true,
Or with His love so deep embrue
Man's sullen heart and gross '
'Jesu, do Thou my soul receive:
Jesu, do Thou my foes forgive;'
He who would learn that prayer must live
Under the holy Cross.

He, though he seem on earth to move,
Must glide in air like gentle dove,
From yon unclouded depths above
Must draw his purer breath;
Till men behold his angel face
All radiant with celestial grace, [13]
Martyr all o'er, and meet to trace
The lines of Jesus' death.

[12] Wheatly on the Common Prayer, c.v. sect. iv. 2. 'As there are three kinds of martyrdom, the first both in will and deed, which is the highest; the second in will but not in deed; the third in

deed but not in will; so the Church commemorates these martyrs in the same order: St. Stephen first, who suffered death both in will and deed; St. John the Evangelist next, who suffered martyrdom in will but not in deed; the holy Innocents last, who suffered in deed but not in will.'

[13] And all that sat in the council, booking steadfastly on him, saw his face as it had been the face of an angel. Acts vi. 15.

ST. JOHN'S DAY

Peter seeing him, saith to Jesus, Lord, and what shall this man do? Jesus saith unto him, If I will that he tarry till I come, what is that to thee? Follow thou Me. St.
John xxi. 21, 22.

'Lord, and what shall this man do?'
Ask'st thou, Christian, for thy friend?
If his love for Christ be true,
Christ hath told thee of his end:
This is he whom God approves,
This is he whom Jesus loves.

Ask not of him more than this,
Leave it in his Saviour's breast,
Whether, early call'd to bliss,
He in youth shall find his rest,
Or armed in his station wait
Till his Lord be at the gate:

Whether in his lonely course
(Lonely, not forlorn) he stay,
Or with Love's supporting force
Cheat the toil, and cheer the way:
Leave it all in His high hand,
Who doth hearts as streams command. [14]

Gales from Heaven, if so He will,

Sweeter melodies can wake
On the lonely mountain rill
Than the meeting waters make.
Who hath the Father and the Son,
May be left, but not alone.

Sick or healthful, slave or free,
Wealthy, or despis'd and poor '
What is that to him or thee,
So his love to Christ endure?
When the shore is won at last,
Who will count the billows past?

Only, since our souls will shrink
At the touch of natural grief,
When our earthly lov'd ones sink,
Lend us, Lord, Thy sure relief;
Patient hearts, their pain to see,
And Thy grace, to follow Thee.

[14] The king's heart is in the hand of the Lord, as the rivers of water: He turneth it whithersoever He will. Proverbs xxi. 1.

THE HOLY INNOCENTS

These were redeemed from among men, being the firstfruits unto
God and to the Lamb. Rev. xiv. 4.

Say, ye celestial guards, who wait
In Bethlehem, round the Saviour's palace gate,
Say, who are these on golden wings,
That hover o'er the new-born King of kings,
Their palms and garlands telling plain
That they are of the glorious martyr-train,
Next to yourselves ordain'd to praise
His Name, and brighten as on Him they gaze?

But where their spoils and trophies? where
The glorious dint a martyr's shield should bear?
How chance no check among them wears
The deep-worn trace of penitential tears,
But all is bright and smiling love,
As if, fresh-borne from Eden's happy grove,
They had flown here, their King to see,
Nor ever had been heirs of dark mortality?

Ask, and some angel will reply,
'These, like yourselves, were born to sin and die,
But ere the poison root was grown,
God set His seal, and mark'd them for His own.
Baptis'd its blood for Jesus' sake,
Now underneath the Cross their bed they make,
Not to be scar'd from that sure rest

By frighten'd mother's shriek, or warrior's waving crest.'

Mindful of these, the firstfruits sweet
Borne by this suffering Church her Lord to greet;
Bless'd Jesus ever lov'd to trace
The 'innocent brightness' of an infant's face.
He rais'd them in His holy arms,
He bless'd them from the world and all its harms:
Heirs though they were of sin and shame,
He bless'd them in his own and in his Father's Name.

Then, as each fond unconscious child
On th' everlasting Parent sweetly smil'd
(Like infants sporting on the shore,
That tremble not at Ocean's boundless roar),
Were they not present to Thy thought,
All souls, that in their cradles Thou hast bought?
But chiefly these, who died for Thee,
That Thou might'st live for them a sadder death to see.

And next to these, Thy gracious word
Was as a pledge of benediction stor'd
For Christian mothers, while they moan
Their treasur'd hopes, just born, baptis'd, and gone.
Oh, joy for Rachel's broken heart!
She and her babes shall meet no more to part;
So dear to Christ her pious haste
To trust them in His arms for ever safe embrac'd.

She dares not grudge to leave them there,
Where to behold them was her heart's first prayer;
She dares not grieve - but she must weep,
As her pale placid martyr sinks to sleep,
Teaching so well and silently
How at the shepherd's call the lamb should die:
How happier far than life the end
Of souls that infant-like beneath their burthen bend.

FIRST SUNDAY AFTER CHRISTMAS

So the sun returned ten degrees, by which degrees it was gone
down. Isaiah xxxviii. 8; compare Josh. x. 13.

'Tis true, of old th' unchanging sun
His daily course refus'd to run,
The pale moon hurrying to the west
Paus'd at a mortal's call, to aid
Th' avenging storm of war, that laid
Seven guilty realms at once on earth's defiled breast.

But can it be, one suppliant tear
Should stay the ever-moving sphere?
A sick man's lowly-breathed sigh,
When from the world he turns away, [15]
And hides his weary eyes to pray,
Should change your mystic dance, ye wanderers of the sky?

We too, O Lord, would fain command,
As then, Thy wonder-working hand,
And backward force the waves of Time,
That now so swift and silent bear
Our restless bark from year to year;
Help us to pause and mourn to Thee our tale of crime.

Bright hopes, that erst the bosom warm'd,
And vows, too pure to be perform'd,
And prayers blown wide by gales of care; -

These, and such faint half-waking dreams,
Like stormy lights on mountain streams,
Wavering and broken all, athwart the conscience glare.

How shall we 'scape the o'erwhelming Past?
Can spirits broken, joys o'ercast,
And eyes that never more may smile: -
Can these th' avenging bolt delay,
Or win us back one little day
The bitterness of death to soften and beguile?

Father and Lover of our souls!
Though darkly round Thine anger rolls,
Thy sunshine smiles beneath the gloom,
Thou seek'st to warn us, not confound,
Thy showers would pierce the harden'd ground
And win it to give out its brightness and perfume.

Thou smil'st on us in wrath, and we,
E'en in remorse, would smile on Thee,
The tears that bathe our offer'd hearts,
We would not have them stain'd and dim,
But dropp'd from wings of seraphim,
All glowing with the light accepted Love imparts.

Time's waters will not ebb, nor stay;
Power cannot change them, but Love may;
What cannot be, Love counts it done.
Deep in the heart, her searching view
Can read where Faith is fix'd and true,
Through shades of setting life can see Heaven's work begun.

O Thou, who keep'st the Key of Love,
Open Thy fount, eternal Dove,
And overflow this heart of mine,
Enlarging as it fills with Thee,
Till in one blaze of charity

Care and remorse are lost, like motes in light divine;

Till as each moment wafts us higher,
By every gush of pure desire,
And high-breath'd hope of joys above,
By every secret sigh we heave,
Whole years of folly we outlive,
In His unerring sight, who measures Life by Love.

[15] Then Hezekiah turned his face toward the wall, and prayed unto the Lord. Isaiah xxxviii. 2.

THE CIRCUMCISION OF CHRIST

In whom also ye are circumcised with the circumcision made
without hands. Coloss. ii. 11.

The year begins with Thee,
And Thou beginn'st with woe,
To let the world of sinners see
That blood for sin must flow.

Thine infant cries, O Lord,
Thy tears upon the breast,
Are not enough - the legal sword
Must do its stern behest.

Like sacrificial wine
Pour'd on a victim's head
Are those few precious drops of Thine,
Now first to offering led.

They are the pledge and seal
Of Christ's unswerving faith
Given to His Sire, our souls to heal,
Although it cost His death.

They to His Church of old,
To each true Jewish heart,
In Gospel graces manifold
Communion blest impart.

Now of Thy love we deem
As of an ocean vast,
Mounting in tides against the stream
Of ages gone and past.

Both theirs and ours Thou art,
As we and they are Thine;
Kings, Prophets, Patriarchs - all have part
Along the sacred line.

By blood and water too
God's mark is set on Thee,
That in Thee every faithful view
Both covenants might see.

O bond of union, dear
And strong as is Thy grace!
Saints, parted by a thousand year,
May thus in heart embrace.

Is there a mourner true,
Who fallen on faithless days,
Sighs for the heart-consoling view
Of those Heaven deign'd to praise?

In spirit may'st thou meet
With faithful Abraham here,
Whom soon in Eden thou shalt greet
A nursing Father dear.

Would'st thou a poet be?
And would thy dull heart fain
Borrow of Israel's minstrelsy
One high enraptured strain?

KEBLE

Come here thy soul to tune,
Here set thy feeble chant,
Here, if at all beneath the moon,
Is holy David's haunt.

Art thou a child of tears,
Cradled in care and woe?
And seems it hard, thy vernal years
Few vernal joys can show?

And fall the sounds of mirth
Sad on thy lonely heart,
From all the hopes and charms of earth
Untimely call'd to part?

Look here, and hold thy peace:
The Giver of all good
E'en from the womb takes no release
From suffering, tears, and blood.

If thou would'st reap in love,
First sow in holy fear:
So life a winter's morn may prove
To a bright endless year.

SECOND SUNDAY AFTER CHRISTMAS

When the poor and needy seek water, and there is none, and
their tongue faileth for thirst, I the Lord will hear them, I the
God of Israel will not forsake them. Isaiah xli. 17.

And wilt thou hear the fever'd heart
To Thee in silence cry?
And as th' inconstant wildfires dart
Out of the restless eye,
Wilt thou forgive the wayward though
By kindly woes yet half untaught
A Saviours right, so dearly bought,
That Hope should never die?

Thou wilt: for many a languid prayer
Has reach'd Thee from the wild,
Since the lorn mother, wandering there,
Cast down her fainting child, [16]
Then stole apart to weep and die,
Nor knew an angel form was nigh,
To show soft waters gushing by,
And dewy shadows mild.

Thou wilt - for Thou art Israel's God,
And Thine unwearied arm
Is ready yet with Moses' rod,
The hidden rill to charm
Out of the dry unfathom'd deep

Of sands, that lie in lifeless sleep,
Save when the scorching whirlwinds heap
Their waves in rude alarm.

These moments of wild wrath are Thine -
Thine, too, the drearier hour
When o'er th' horizon's silent line
Fond hopeless fancies cower,
And on the traveller's listless way
Rises and sets th' unchanging day,
No cloud in heaven to slake its ray,
On earth no sheltering bower.

Thou wilt be there, and not forsake,
To turn the bitter pool
Into a bright and breezy lake,
This throbbing brow to cool:
Till loft awhile with Thee alone
The wilful heart be fain to own
That He, by whom our bright hours shone,
Our darkness best may rule.

The scent of water far away
Upon the breeze is flung;
The desert pelican to-day
Securely leaves her young,
Reproving thankless man, who fears
To journey on a few lone years,
Where on the sand Thy step appears,
Thy crown in sight is hung.

Thou, who did sit on Jacob's well
The weary hour of noon, [17]
The languid pulses Thou canst tell,
The nerveless spirit tune.
Thou from Whose cross in anguish burst
The cry that owned Thy dying thirst, [18]

46

To Thee we turn, our Last and First,
Our Sun and soothing Moon.

From darkness, here, and dreariness
We ask not full repose,
Only be Thou at hand, to bless
Our trial hour of woes.
Is not the pilgrim's toil o'erpaid
By the clear rill and palmy shade?
And see we not, up Earth's dark glade,
The gate of Heaven unclose?

[16] Hagar. See Genesis xxi. 15.
[17] St. John iv. 6.
[18] St. John xix. 28.

THE EPIPHANY

And lo, the star, which they saw in the east, went before them,
till it came and stood over where the young Child was. When
they saw the star, they rejoiced with exceeding great joy.
St. Matthew ii. 9, 10.

Star of the East, how sweet art Thou,
Seen in life's early morning sky,
Ere yet a cloud has dimm'd the brow,
While yet we gaze with childish eye;

When father, mother, nursing friend,
Most dearly lov'd, and loving best,
First bid us from their arms ascend,
Pointing to Thee, in Thy sure rest.

Too soon the glare of earthly day
Buries, to us, Thy brightness keen,
And we are left to find our way
By faith and hope in Thee unseen.

What matter? if the waymarks sure
On every side are round us set,
Soon overleap'd, but not obscure?
'Tis ours to mark them or forget.

What matter? if in calm old age
Our childhood's star again arise,
Crowning our lonely pilgrimage

With all that cheers a wanderer's eyes?

Ne'er may we lose it from our sight,
Till all our hopes and thoughts are led
   To where it stays its lucid flight
   Over our Saviour's lowly bed.

There, swath'd in humblest poverty,
   On Chastity's meek lap enshrin'd,
With breathless Reverence waiting by,
When we our Sovereign Master find,

   Will not the long-forgotten glow
   Of mingled joy and awe return,
When stars above or flowers below
First made our infant spirits burn?

Look on us, Lord, and take our parts
   E'en on Thy throne of purity!
From these our proud yet grovelling hearts
Hide not Thy mild forgiving eye.

Did not the Gentile Church find grace,
   Our mother dear, this favoured day?
With gold and myrrh she sought Thy face;
Nor didst Thou turn Thy face away.

She too, [19] in earlier, purer days,
Had watched thee gleaming faint and far '
But wandering in self-chosen ways
She lost Thee quite, Thou lovely star.

Yet had her Father's finger turn'd
To Thee her first inquiring glance:
The deeper shame within her burn'd,
When waken'd from her wilful trance.

Behold, her wisest throng Thy gate,
Their richest, sweetest, purest store,
(Yet own'd too worthless and too late,)
They lavish on Thy cottage-floor.

They give their best - O tenfold shame
On us their fallen progeny,
Who sacrifice the blind and lame [20] -
Who will not wake or fast with Thee!

[19] The Patriarchal Church.
[20] Malachi i. 8.

FIRST SUNDAY AFTER EPIPHANY

They shall spring up as among the grass, as willows by the water courses. Isaiah xliv. 4.

Lessons sweet of spring returning,
Welcome to the thoughtful heart!
May I call ye sense or learning,
Instinct pure, or Heaven-taught art?
Be your title what it may,
Sweet this lengthening April day,
While with you the soul is free,
Ranging wild o-er hill and lea.

Soft as Memnon's harp at morning,
To the inward ear devout,
Touch'd by light, with heavenly warning
Your transporting chords ring out.
Every leaf in every nook,
Every wave in every brook,
Chanting with a solemn voice,
Minds us of our better choice.

Needs no show of mountain hoary,
Winding shore or deepening glen,
Where the landscape in its glory
Teaches truth to wandering men:
Give true hearts but earth and sky,
And some flowers to bloom and die,
Homely scenes and simple views

Lowly thoughts may best infuse.

See the soft green willow springing
Where the waters gently pass,
Every way her free arms flinging
O'er the moist and reedy grass.
Long ere winter blasts are fled,
See her tipp'd with vernal red,
And her kindly flower displayed
Ere her leaf can cast a shade.

Though the rudest hand assail her,
Patiently she droops awhile,
But when showers and breezes hail her,
Wears again her willing smile.
Thus I learn Contentment's power
From the slighted willow bower,
Ready to give thanks and live
On the least that Heaven may give.

If, the quiet brooklet leaving,
Up the stony vale I wind,
Haply half in fancy grieving
For the shades I leave behind,
By the dusty wayside drear,
Nightingales with joyous cheer
Sing, my sadness to reprove,
Gladlier than in cultured grove.

Where the thickest boughs are twining
Of the greenest darkest tree,
There they plunge, the light declining -
All may hear, but none may see.
Fearless of the passing hoof,
Hardly will they fleet aloof;
So they live in modest ways,
Trust entire, and ceaseless praise.

SECOND SUNDAY AFTER EPIPHANY

Every man at the beginning doth set forth good wine: and when
men have well drunk, then that which is worse; but thou hast
kept the good wine until now.
St. John ii. 10.

The heart of childhood is all mirth:
We frolic to and fro
As free and blithe, as if on earth
Were no such thing as woe.

But if indeed with reckless faith
We trust the flattering voice,
Which whispers, "Take thy fill ere death,
Indulge thee and rejoice;"

Too surely, every setting day,
Some lost delight we mourn;
The flowers all die along our way
Till we, too, die forlorn.

Such is the world's gay garish feast,
In her first charming bowl
Infusing all that fires the breast,
And cheats the unstable soul.

And still, as loud the revel swells,
The fever'd pulse beats higher,

Till the sear'd taste from foulest wells
Is fain to slake its fire.

Unlike the feast of heavenly love
Spread at the Saviour's word
For souls that hear His call, and prove
Meet for His bridal board.

Why should we fear, youth's draught of joy
If pure would sparkle less?
Why should the cup the sooner cloy,
Which God hath deign'd to bless?

For, is it Hope, that thrills so keen
Along each bounding vein,
Still whispering glorious things unseen? -
Faith makes the vision plain.

The world would kill her soon: but Faith
Her daring dreams will cherish,
Speeding her gaze o'er time and death
To realms where nought can perish.

Or is it Love, the dear delight
Of hearts that know no guile,
That all around see all things bright
With their own magic smile?

The silent joy that sinks so deep,
Of confidence and rest,
Lull'd in a father's arms to sleep,
Clasp'd to a mother's breast?

Who, but a Christian, through all life
That blessing may prolong?
Who, through the world's sad day of strife,
Still chant his morning song?

Fathers may hate us or forsake,
God's foundlings then are we:
Mother on child no pity take, [21]
But we shall still have Thee.

We may look home, and seek in vain
A fond fraternal heart,
But Christ hath given His promise plain
To do a Brother's part.

Nor shall dull age, as worldlings say,
The heavenward flame annoy:
The Saviour cannot pass away,
And with Him lives our joy.

Ever the richest, tenderest glow
Sets round the autumnal sun -
But there sight fails: no heart may know
The bliss when life is done.

Such is Thy banquet, dearest Lord;
O give us grace, to cast
Our lot with Thine, to trust Thy word,
And keep our best till last.

[21] Can a woman forget her sucking child, that she should not
have compassion on the son of her womb? yea, they may forget,
yet will I not forget thee. Isaiah xlix. 15.

THIRD SUNDAY AFTER EPIPHANY

When Jesus heard it, He marvelled, and said to them that fol-
lowed, Verily I say unto you, I have not found so great faith, no,
not in Israel.
St.Matthew viii. 10.

I mark'd a rainbow in the north,
What time the wild autumnal sun
From his dark veil at noon look'd forth,
As glorying in his course half done,
Flinging soft radiance far and wide
Over the dusky heaven and bleak hill-side.

It was a gleam to Memory dear,
And as I walk and muse apart,
When all seems faithless round and drear,
I would revive it in my heart,
And watch how light can find its way
To regions farthest from the fount of day.

Light flashes in the gloomiest sky,
And Music in the dullest plain,
For there the lark is soaring high
Over her flat and leafless reign,
And chanting in so blithe a tone,
It shames the weary heart to feel itself alone.

Brighter than rainbow in the north,

More cheery than the matin lark,
Is the soft gleam of Christian worth,
Which on some holy house we mark;
Dear to the pastor's aching heart
To think, where'er he looks, such gleam may have a part;

May dwell, unseen by all but Heaven,
Like diamond blazing in the mine;
For ever, where such grace is given,
It fears in open day to shine, [22]
Lest the deep stain it owns within
Break out, and Faith be sham'd by the believer's sin.

In silence and afar they wait,
To find a prayer their Lord may hear:
Voice of the poor and desolate,
You best may bring it to His ear;
Your grateful intercessions rise
With more than royal pomp, and pierce the skies.

Happy the soul whose precious cause
You in the Sovereign Presence plead -
"This is the lover of Thy laws, [23]
The friend of Thine in fear and need," -
For to the poor Thy mercy lends
That solemn style, "Thy nation and Thy friends."

He too is blest whose outward eye
The graceful lines of art may trace,
While his free spirit, soaring high,
Discerns the glorious from the base;
Till out of dust his magic raise [24]
A home for prayer and love, and full harmonious praise,

Where far away and high above,
In maze on maze the tranced sight
Strays, mindful of that heavenly love

Which knows no end in depth or height,
While the strong breath of Music seems
To waft us ever on, soaring in blissful dreams.

What though in poor and humble guise
Thou here didst sojourn, cottage-born?
Yet from Thy glory in the skies
Our earthly gold Thou dost not scorn.
For Love delights to bring her best,
And where Love is, that offering evermore is blest.

Love on the Saviour's dying head
Her spikenard drops unblam'd may pour,
May mount His cross, and wrap Him dead
In spices from the golden shore; [25]
Risen, may embalm His sacred name
With all a Painter's art, and all a Minstrel's flame.

Worthless and lost our offerings seem,
Drops in the ocean of His praise;
But Mercy with her genial beam
Is ripening them to pearly blaze,
To sparkle in His crown above,
Who welcomes here a child's as there an angel's love.

[22] Lord, I am not worthy that Thou shouldest enter under my roof. St. Luke vii. 6. "From the first time that the impressions of religion settled deeply in his mind, he used great caution to conceal it; not only in obedience to the rule given by our Saviour, of fasting, prayer, and giving alm in secret, but from a particular distrust he had of himself; for he said, he was afraid that he should at some time or other do some enormous thing, which, if he were looked on as a very religious man, might cast a reproach on the profession of it, and give great disadvantage to impious men to blaspheme the name of God." Burnet's Life of Hale, in Wordsworth's Eccl. Biog. vi. 73.
[23] He loveth our nation. St. Luke vii. 5.

[24] He hath built us a synagogue. St. Luke vii. 5.
[25] St. John xii. 7; xix. 30,

FOURTH SUNDAY AFTER EPIPHANY

When they saw Him, they besought Him that He would depart
out of their coasts. St. Matthew viii. 34.

They know the Almighty's power,
Who, waken'd by the rushing midnight shower,
Watch for the fitful breeze
To howl and chafe amid the bending trees,
Watch for the still white gleam
To bathe the landscape in a fiery stream,
Touching the tremulous eye with sense of light
Too rapid and too pure for all but angel sight.

They know the Almighty's love,
Who, when the whirlwinds rock the topmost grove,
Stand in the shade, and hear
The tumult with a deep exulting fear,
How, in their fiercest sway,
Curb'd by some power unseen, they die away,
Like a bold steed that owns his rider's arm,
Proud to be check'd and sooth'd by that o'er-mastering chains.

But there are storms within
That heave the struggling heart with wilder din,
And there is power and love
The maniac's rushing frenzy to reprove,
And when he takes his seat,
Cloth'd and in calmness, at his Savour's feet, [26]

Is not the power as strange, the love as blest,
As when He said, "Be still," and ocean sank to rest?

Woe to the wayward heart,
That gladlier turns to eye the shuddering start
Of Passion in her might,
Than marks the silent growth of grace and light; -
Pleas'd in the cheerless tomb
To linger, while the morning rays illume
Green lake, and cedar tuft, and spicy glade,
Shaking their dewy tresses now the storm is laid.

The storm is laid - and now
In His meek power He climbs the mountain's brow,
Who bade the waves go sleep,
And lash'd the vex'd fiends to their yawning deep.
How on a rock they stand,
Who watch His eye, and hold His guiding hand!
Not half so fix'd, amid her vassal hills,
Rises the holy pile that Kedron's valley fills.

And wilt thou seek again
Thy howling waste, thy charnel-house and chain,
And with the demons be,
Rather than clasp thine own Deliverer's knee?
Sure 'tis no Heaven-bred awe
That bids thee from His healing touch withdraw;
The world and He are struggling in thine heart,
And in thy reckless mood thou bidd'st thy Lord depart.

He, merciful and mild,
As erst, beholding, loves His wayward child;
When souls of highest birth
Waste their impassion'd might on dreams of earth,
He opens Nature's book,
And on His glorious Gospel bids them look,
Till, by such chords as rule the choirs above,

Their lawless cries are tun'd to hymns of perfect love.

[26] St. Mark v. 15; iv. 39.

FIFTH SUNDAY AFTER EPIPHANY

Behold, the Lord's hand is not shortened, that it cannot save;
neither His ear heavy, that it cannot hear; but your iniquities
have separated between you and your God.
Isaiah lix. 1, 2.

'Wake, arm Divine! awake,
Eye of the only Wise!
Now for Thy glory's sake,
Saviour and God, arise,
And may Thine ear, that sealed seems,
In pity mark our mournful themes!'

Thus in her lonely hour
Thy Church is fain to cry,
As if Thy love and power
Were vanish'd from her sky;
Yet God is there, and at His side
He triumphs, who for sinners died.

Ah! 'tis the world enthralls
The Heaven-betrothed breast:
The traitor Sense recalls
The soaring soul from rest.
That bitter sigh was all for earth,
For glories gone and vanish'd mirth.

Age would to youth return,

Farther from Heaven would be,
To feel the wildfire burn,
On idolising knee
Again to fall, and rob Thy shrine
Of hearts, the right of Love Divine.

Lord of this erring flock!
Thou whose soft showers distil
On ocean waste or rock,
Free as on Hermon hill,
Do Thou our craven spirits cheer,
And shame away the selfish tear.

'Twas silent all and dead [27]
Beside the barren sea,
Where Philip's steps were led,
Led by a voice from Thee '
He rose and went, nor ask'd Thee why,
Nor stay'd to heave one faithless sigh:

Upon his lonely way
The high-born traveller came,
Reading a mournful lay
Of 'One who bore our shame, [28]
Silent Himself, His name untold,
And yet His glories were of old.'

To muse what Heaven might mean
His wondering brow he rais'd,
And met an eye serene
That on him watchful gaz'd.
No Hermit e'er so welcome cross'd
A child's lone path in woodland lost.

Now wonder turns to love;
The scrolls of sacred lore
No darksome mazes prove;

THE CHRISTIAN YEAR

The desert tires no more
They bathe where holy waters flow,
Then on their way rejoicing go.

They part to meet in Heaven;
But of the joy they share,
Absolving and forgiven,
The sweet remembrance bear.
Yes - mark him well, ye cold and proud.
Bewilder'd in a heartless crowd,

Starting and turning pale
At Rumour's angry din '
No storm can now assail
The charm he wears within,
Rejoicing still, and doing good,
And with the thought of God imbu'd.

No glare of high estate,
No gloom of woe or want,
The radiance can abate
Where Heaven delights to haunt:
Sin only bides the genial ray,
And, round the Cross, makes night of day.

Then weep it from thy heart;
So mayst thou duly learn
The intercessor's part;
Thy prayers and tears may earn
For fallen souls some healing breath,
Era they have died th' Apostate's death.

[27] See Acts viii. 26-40.
[28] Isaiah liii. 6-8.

SIXTH SUNDAY AFTER EPIPHANY

Beloved, now are we the sons of God, and it doth not yet appear
what we shall be: but we know that, when He shall appear, we
shall be like Him; for we shall see Him as he is.
1 St. John iii. 2.

There are, who darkling and alone,
Would wish the weary night were gone,
Though dawning morn should only show
The secret of their unknown woe:
Who pray for sharpest throbs of pain
To ease them of doubt's galling chain:
'Only disperse the cloud,' they cry,
'And if our fate be death, give light and let us die.' [29]

Unwise I deem them, Lord, unmeet
To profit by Thy chastenings sweet,
For Thou wouldst have us linger still
Upon the verge of good or ill.
That on Thy guiding hand unseen
Our undivided hearts may lean,
And this our frail and foundering bark
Glide in the narrow wake of Thy beloved ark.

'Tis so in war - the champion true
Loves victory more when dim in view
He sees her glories gild afar
The dusky edge of stubborn war,

Than if th' untrodden bloodless field
The harvest of her laurels yield;
Let not my bark in calm abide,
But win her fearless way against the chafing tide.

'Tis so in love - the faithful heart
From her dim vision would not part,
When first to her fond gaze is given
That purest spot in Fancy's heaven,
For all the gorgeous sky beside,
Though pledg'd her own and sure t' abide:
Dearer than every past noon-day
That twilight gleam to her, though faint and far away.

So have I seen some tender flower
Priz'd above all the vernal bower,
Shelter'd beneath the coolest shade,
Embosom'd in the greenest glade,
So frail a gem, it scarce may bear
The playful touch of evening air;
When hardier grown we love it less,
And trust it from our sight, not needing our caress.

And wherefore is the sweet spring-tide
Worth all the changeful year beside?
The last-born babe, why lies its part
Deep in the mother's inmost heart?
But that the Lord and Source of love
Would have His weakest ever prove
Our tenderest care - and most of all
Our frail immortal souls, His work and Satan's thrall.

So be it, Lord; I know it best,
Though not as yet this wayward breast
Beat quite in answer to Thy voice,
Yet surely I have made my choice;
I know not yet the promis'd bliss,

Know not if I shall win or miss;
So doubting, rather let me die,
Than close with aught beside, to last eternally.

What is the Heaven we idly dream?
The self-deceiver's dreary theme,
A cloudless sun that softly shines,
Bright maidens and unfailing vines,
The warrior's pride, the hunter's mirth,
Poor fragments all of this low earth:
Such as in sleep would hardly soothe
A soul that once had tasted of immortal Truth.

What is the Heaven our God bestows?
No Prophet yet, no Angel knows;
Was never yet created eye
Could see across Eternity;
Not seraph's wing for ever soaring
Can pass the flight of souls adoring,
That nearer still and nearer grow
To th' unapproached Lord, once made for them so low.

Unseen, unfelt their earthly growth,
And self-accus'd of sin and sloth,
They live and die; their names decay,
Their fragrance passes quite away;
Like violets in the freezing blast
No vernal steam around they cast. '
But they shall flourish from the tomb,
The breath of God shall wake them into odorous bloom.

Then on th' incarnate Saviour's breast,
The fount of sweetness, they shall rest,
Their spirits every hour imbu'd
More deeply with His precious blood.
But peace - still voice and closed eye
Suit best with hearts beyond the sky,

Hearts training in their low abode,
Daily to lose themselves in hope to find their God.

[29] En de faci xai olesson.

SEPTUAGESIMA SUNDAY

The invisible things of Him from the creation of the world are
clearly seen, being understood by the things that are made.
Romans i. 20.

There is a book, who runs may read,
Which heavenly truth imparts,
And all the lore its scholars need,
Pure eyes and Christian hearts.

The works of God above, below,
Within us and around,
Are pages in that book, to show
How God Himself is found.

The glorious sky embracing all
Is like the Maker's love,
Wherewith encompass'd, great and small
In peace and order move.

The Moon above, the Church below,
A wondrous race they run,
But all their radiance, all their glow,
Each borrows of its Sun.

The Savour lends the light and heat
That crowns His holy hill;
The saints, like stars, around His seat

Perform their courses still. [30]

The saints above are stars in heaven '
What are the saints on earth?
Like tress they stand whom God has given, [31]
Our Eden's happy birth.

Faith is their fix'd unswerving root,
Hope their unfading flower,
Fair deeds of charity their fruit,
The glory of their bower.

The dew of heaven is like Thy grace, [32]
It steals in silence down;
But where it lights, this favour'd place
By richest fruits is known.

One Name above all glorious names
With its ten thousand tongues
The everlasting sea proclaims.
Echoing angelic songs.

The raging Fire, [33] the roaring Wind,
Thy boundless power display;
But in the gentler breeze we find
Thy Spirit's viewless way. [34]

Two worlds are ours: 'tis only Sin
Forbids us to descry
The mystic heaven and earth within,
Plain as the sea and sky.

Thou, who hast given me eyes to see
And love this sight so fair,
Give me a heart to find out Thee,
And read Thee everywhere.

[30] Daniel xii. 3.
[31] Isaiah lx. 21.
[32] Psalm lxviii. 9.
[33] Hebrews xii. 29.
[34] St. John iii. 8.

SEXAGESIMA SUNDAY

Insert section break here

So He drove out the man; and He placed at the east of the garden
of Eden Cherubims, and a flaming sword which turned every
way, to keep the way of the tree of life. Genesis iii. 24; compare
chap. vi.

Foe of mankind! too bold thy race:
Thou runn'st at such a reckless pace,
Thine own dire work thou surely wilt confound:
'Twas but one little drop of sin
We saw this morning enter in,
And lo! at eventide the world is drown'd.

See here the fruit of wandering eyes,
Of worldly longings to be wise,
Of Passion dwelling on forbidden sweets:
Ye lawless glances, freely rove;
Ruin below and wrath above
Are all that now the wildering fancy meets.

Lord, when in some deep garden glade,
Of Thee and of myself afraid.
From thoughts like these among the bowers I hide,
Nearest and loudest then of all
I seem to hear the Judge's call: '
'Where art thou, fallen man? come forth, and be thou tried.'

Trembling before Thee as I stand,
Where'er I gaze on either hand
The sentence is gone forth, the ground is curs'd:
Yet mingled with the penal shower
Some drops of balm in every bower
Steal down like April dews, that softest fall and first.

If filial and maternal love [35]
Memorial of our guilt must prove,
If sinful babes in sorrow must be born,
Yet, to assuage her sharpest throes,
The faithful mother surely knows,
This was the way Thou cam'st to save the world forlorn.

If blessed wedlock may not bless [36]
Without some tinge of bitterness
To dash her cup of joy, since Eden lost,
Chaining to earth with strong desire
Hearts that would highest else aspire,
And o'er the tenderer sex usurping ever most;

Yet by the light of Christian lore
'Tis blind Idolatry no more,
But a sweet help and pattern of true love,
Showing how best the soul may cling
To her immortal Spouse and King,
How He should rule, and she with full desire approve.

If niggard Earth her treasures hide, [37]
To all but labouring hands denied,
Lavish of thorns and worthless weeds alone,
The doom is half in mercy given,
To train us in our way to Heaven,
And show our lagging souls how glory must be won.

If on the sinner's outward frame [38]

God hath impressed His mark of blame,
And e'en our bodies shrink at touch of light,
Yet mercy hath not left us bare:
The very weeds we daily wear [39]
Are to Faith's eye a pledge of God's forgiving might.

And oh! if yet one arrow more, [40]
The sharpest of th'Almighty's store,
Tremble upon the string - a sinner's death '
Art Thou not by to soothe and save,
To lay us gently in the grave,
To close the weary eye and hush the parting breath?

Therefore in sight of man bereft
The happy garden still was left;
The fiery sword that guarded, show'd it too;
Turning all ways, the world to teach,
That though as yet beyond our reach,
Still in its place the tree of life and glory grew.

[35] In sorrow thou shalt bring forth children.
[36] Thy desie shall be to thy husband, and he shall rule over thee.
[37] Cursed is the ground for thy sake.
[38] I was afraid, because I was naked.
[39] The Lord God made coats of skins, and clothed them.
[40] Thou shalt surely die.

QUINQUAGESIMA SUNDAY

I do set My bow in the cloud, and it shall be for a token of a covenant between Me and the earth. Genesis ix. 13.

Sweet Dove! the softest, steadiest plume,
In all the sunbright sky,
Brightening in ever-changeful bloom
As breezes change on high; -

Sweet Leaf! the pledge of peace and mirth,
'Long sought, and lately won,'
Bless'd increase of reviving Earth,
When first it felt the Sun; -

Sweet Rainbow! pride of summer days,
High set at Heaven's command,
Though into drear and dusky haze
Thou melt on either hand; -

Dear tokens of a pardoning God,
We hail ye, one and all,
As when our fathers walk'd abroad,
Freed from their twelvemonth's thrall.

How joyful from th'imprisoning ark
On the green earth they spring!
Not blither, after showers, the lark

Mounts up with glistening wing.

So home-bound sailors spring to shore,
Two oceans safely past;
So happy souls, when life is o'er,
Plunge in th'empyreal vast.

What wins their first and fondest gaze
In all the blissful field,
And keeps it through a thousand days?
Love face to face reveal'd:

Love imag'd in that cordial look
Our Lord in Eden bends
On souls that sin and earth forsook
In time to die His friends.

And what most welcome and serene
Dawns on the Patriarch's eye,
In all the emerging hills so green,
In all the brightening sky?

What but the gentle rainbow's gleam,
Soothing the wearied sight,
That cannot bear the solar beam,
With soft undazzling light?

Lord, if our fathers turn'd to Thee
With such adoring gaze,
Wondering frail man Thy light should see
Without Thy scorching blaze;

Where is our love, and where our hearts,
We who have seen Thy Son,
Have tried Thy Spirit's winning arts,
And yet we are not won?

KEBLE

The Son of God in radiance beam'd
Too bright for us to scan,
But we may face the rays that stream'd
From the mild Son of Man.

There, parted into rainbow hues,
In sweet harmonious strife
We see celestial love diffuse
Its light o'er Jesus' life.

God, by His bow, vouchsafes to write
This truth in Heaven above:
As every lovely hue is Light,
So every grace is Love.

ASH WEDNESDAY

When thou fastest, anoint thine head, and wash thy face; that
thou appear not unto men to fast, but unto thy Father which is in
secret. St. Matthew vi. 17, 18.

'Yes - deep within and deeper yet
The rankling shaft of conscience hide,
Quick let the swelling eye forget
The tears that in the heart abide.
Calm be the voice, the aspect bold,
No shuddering pass o'er lip or brow,
For why should Innocence be told
The pangs that guilty spirits bow?

'The loving eye that watches thine
Close as the air that wraps thee round '
Why in thy sorrow should it pine,
Since never of thy sin it found?
And wherefore should the heathen see [41]
What chains of darkness thee enslave,
And mocking say, 'Lo, this is he
Who own'd a God that could not save'?'

Thus oft the mourner's wayward heart
Tempts him to hide his grief and die,
Too feeble for Confession's smart,
Too proud to bear a pitying eye;

How sweet, in that dark hour, to fall
On bosoms waiting to receive
Our sighs, and gently whisper all!
They love us - will not God forgive?

Else let us keep our fast within,
Till Heaven and we are quite alone,
Then let the grief, the shame, the sin,
Before the mercy-seat be thrown.
Between the porch and altar weep,
Unworthy of the holiest place,
Yet hoping near the shrine to keep
One lowly cell in sight of grace.

Nor fear lest sympathy should fail '
Hast thou not seen, in night hours drear,
When racking thoughts the heart assail,
The glimmering stars by turns appear,
And from the eternal house above
With silent news of mercy steal?
So Angels pause on tasks of love,
To look where sorrowing sinners kneel.

Or if no Angel pass that way,
He who in secret sees, perchance
May bid His own heart-warming ray
Toward thee stream with kindlier glance,
As when upon His drooping head
His Father's light was pour'd from Heaven,
What time, unshelter'd and unfed, [42]
Far in the wild His steps were driven.

High thoughts were with Him in that hour,
Untold, unspeakable on earth '
And who can stay the soaring power
Of spirits wean'd from worldly mirth,
While far beyond the sound of praise

With upward eye they float serene,
And learn to bear their Saviour's blaze
When Judgment shall undraw the screen?

[41] Wherefore should they say among the people, Where is their
God? Joel ii. 17.
[42] St. Matthew iv. 1.

FIRST SUNDAY IN LENT

Haste thee, escape thither: for I cannot do any thing till thou be
come thither. Therefore the name of the city was called Zoar.
Genesis xix. 22.

'Angel of wrath! why linger in mid-air,
While the devoted city's cry
Louder and louder swells? and canst thou spare,
Thy full charg'd vial standing by?'
Thus, with stern voice, unsparing Justice pleads:
He hears her not - with soften'd gaze
His eye is following where sweet Mercy leads,
And till she give the sign, his fury stays.

Guided by her, along the mountain road,
Far through the twilight of the morn,
With hurrying footsteps from thÃ© accurs'd abode
He sees the holy household borne;
Angels, or more, on either hand are nigh,
To speed them o'er the tempting plain,
Lingering in heart, and with frail sidelong eye
Seeking how near they may unharm'd remain.

'Ah! wherefore gleam those upland slopes so fair?
And why, through every woodland arch,
Swells yon bright vale, as Eden rich and rare,
Where Jordan winds his stately march;

If all must be forsaken, ruin'd all,
If God have planted but to burn? '
Surely not yet th'avenging shower will fall,
Though to my home for one last look I turn.'

Thus while they waver, surely long ago
They had provok'd the withering blast,
But that the merciful Avengers know
Their frailty well, and hold them fast.
'Haste, for thy life escape, nor look behind''
Ever in thrilling sounds like these
They check the wandering eye, severely kind,
Nor let the sinner lose his soul at ease.

And when, o'erwearied with the steep ascent,
We for a nearer refuge crave,
One little spot of ground in mercy lent,
One hour of home before the grave,
Oft in His pity o'er His children weak,
His hand withdraws the penal fire,
And where we fondly cling, forbears to wreak
Full vengeance, till our hearts are wean'd entire.

Thus, by the merits of one righteous man,
The Church, our Zoar, shall abide,
Till she abuse, so sore, her lengthen'd span,
E'en Mercy's self her face must hide.
Then, onward yet a step, thou hard-won soul;
Though in the Church thou know thy place,
The mountain farther lies - there seek thy goal,
There breathe at large, o'erpast thy dangerous race.

Sweet is the smile of home; the mutual look
When hearts are of each other sure;
Sweet all the joys that crowd the household nook,
The haunt of all affections pure;
Yet in the world e'en these abide, and we

Above the world our calling boast;
Once gain the mountain-top, and thou art free:
Till then, who rest, presume; who turn to look, are lost.

SECOND SUNDAY IN LENT

And when Esau heard the words of his father, he cried with a great and exceeding bitter cry, and said unto his father, Bless me, even me also, O my father. Genesis xxvii. 34. (Compare Hebrews xii. 17. He found no place of repentance, though he sought it carefully with tears. [43])

'And is there in God's world so drear a place
Where the loud bitter cry is rais'd in vain?
Where tears of penance come too late for grace,
As on th'uprooted flower the genial rain?'

'Tis even so: the sovereign Lord of souls
Stores in the dungeon of His boundless realm
Each bolt that o'er the sinner vainly rolls,
With gather'd wrath the reprobate to whelm.

Will the storm hear the sailor's piteous cry, [44]
Taught so mistrust, too late, the tempting wave,
When all around he sees but sea and sky,
A God in anger, a self-chosen grave?

Or will the thorns, that strew intemperance'bed,
Turn with a wish to down? will late remorse
Recall the shaft the murderer's hand has sped,
Or from the guiltless bosom turn its course?

Then may the unbodied soul in safety fleet

Through the dark curtains of the world above,
Fresh from the stain of crime; nor fear to meet
The God whom here she would not learn to love;

Then is there hope for such as die unblest,
That angel wings may waft them to the shore,
Nor need th'unready virgin strike her breast,
Nor wait desponding round the bridegroom's door.

But where is then the stay of contrite hearts?
Of old they lean'd on Thy eternal word,
But with the sinner's fear their hope departs,
Fast link'd as Thy great Name to Thee, O Lord:

That Name, by which Thy faithful oath is past,
That we should endless be, for joy or woe: '
And if the treasures of Thy wrath could waste,
Thy lovers must their promis'd Heaven forego.

But ask of elder days, earth's vernal hour,
When in familiar talk God's voice was heard,
When at the Patriarch's call the fiery shower
Propitious o'er the turf-built shrine appear'd.

Watch by our father Isaac's pastoral door '
The birthright sold, the blessing lost and won;
Tell, Heaven has wrath that can relent no more;
The Grave, dark deeds that cannot be undone.

We barter life for pottage; sell true bliss
For wealth or power, for pleasure or renown;
Thus, Esau-like, our Father's blessing miss,
Then wash with fruitless tears our faded crown.

Our faded crown, despis'd and flung aside,
Shall on some brother's brow immortal bloom;
No partial hand the blessing may misguide,

No flattering fancy change our Monarch's doom:

His righteous doom, that meek true-hearted Love
    The everlasting birthright should receive,
    The softest dews drop on her from above, [45]
    The richest green her mountain garland weave:

    Her brethren, mightiest, wisest, eldest-born,
    Bow to her sway, and move at her behest;
    Isaac's fond blessing may not fall on scorn,
Nor Balaam's curse on Love, which God hath blest.

[43] The author earnestly hopes, that nothing in these stanzas will be understood to express any opinion as to the general efficacy of what is called 'a death-bed repentance.' Such questions are best left in the merciful obscurity with which Scripture has enveloped them. Esau's probation, as far as his birthright was concerned, was quite over when he uttered the cry in the text. His despondency, therefore, is not parallel to anything on this side of the grave.

[44] Compare Bp. Butler's Analogy, p. 54-64, ed. 1736.

[45] Genesis xxvii. 27, 28.

THIRD SUNDAY IN LENT

When a strong man armed keepeth his place, his goods are in peace; but when a stronger than he shall come upon him, and overcome him, he taketh from him all his armour wherein he trusted, and divideth his spoils.
St. Luke xi. 21,22.

See Lucifer like lightning fall,
Dash'd from his throne of pride;
While, answering Thy victorious call,
The Saints his spoils divide;
This world of Thine, by him usurp'd too long,
Now opening all her stores to heal Thy servants'wrong.

So when the first-born of Thy foes
Dead in the darkness lay,
When Thy redeem'd at midnight rose
And cast their bonds away,
The orphan'd realm threw wide her gates, and told
Into freed Israel's lap her jewels and her gold.

And when their wondrous march was o'er,
And they had won their homes,
Where Abraham fed his flock of yore,
Among their fathers'tombs; -
A land that drinks the rain of Heaven at will,
Whose waters kiss the feet of many a vine-clad hill; -

Oft as they watch'd, at thoughtful eve,
A gale from bowers of balm
Sweep o'er the billowy corn, and heave
The tresses of the palm,
Just as the lingering Sun had touch'd with gold,
Far o'er the cedar shade, some tower of giants old;

It was a fearful joy, I ween,
To trace the Heathen's toil,
The limpid wells, the orchards green,
Left ready for the spoil,
The household stores untouch'd, the roses bright
Wreath'd o'er the cottage walls in garlands of delight.

And now another Canaan yields
To Thine all-conquering ark: '
Fly from the 'old poetic' fields, [46]
Ye Paynim shadows dark!
Immortal Greece, dear land of glorious lays,
Lo! here the 'unknown God' of thy unconscious praise.

The olive-wreath, the ivied wand,
'The sword in myrtles drest,.'
Each legend of the shadowy strand
Now wakes a vision blest;
As little children lisp, and tell of Heaven,
So thoughts beyond their thought to those high Bards were
given.

And these are ours: Thy partial grace
The tempting treasure lends:
These relies of a guilty race
Are forfeit to Thy friends;
What seem'd an idol hymn, now breathes of Thee,
Tun'd by Faith's ear to some celestial melody.

There's not a strain to Memory dear,

Nor flower in classic grove,
There's not a sweet note warbled here,
But minds us of Thy Love.
O Lord, our Lord, and spoiler of our foes,
There is no light but Thine: with Thee all beauty glows.

[46] Where each old poetic mountain Inspiration breathed around.
Gray.

FOURTH SUNDAY IN LENT

Joseph made haste; - or his bowels did yearn upon his brother;
and he sought where to weep, and he entered into his chamber
and wept there. Genesis xliii. 30.
There stood no man with him, while Joseph made himself
known unto his brethren. Genesis xlv. 1.

When Nature tries her finest touch,
Weaving her vernal wreath,
Mark ye, how close she veils her round,
Not to be trac'd by sight or sound,
Nor soil'd by ruder breath?

Who ever saw the earliest rose
First open her sweet breast?
Or, when the summer sun goes down,
The first soft star in evening's crown
Light up her gleaming crest?

Fondly we seek the dawning bloom
On features wan and fair,
The gazing eye no change can trace,
But look away a little space,
Then turn, and lo! 'tis there.

But there's a sweeter flower than e'er
Blush'd on the rosy spray '
A brighter star, a richer bloom

Than e'er did western heaven illume
At close of summer day.

'Tis Love, the last best gift of Heaven;
Love gentle, holy, pure;
But tenderer than a dove's soft eye,
The searching sun, the open sky,
She never could endure.

E'en human Love will shrink from sight
Here in the coarse rude earth:
How then should rash intruding glance
Break in upon her sacred trance
Who boasts a heavenly birth?

So still and secret is her growth,
Ever the truest heart,
Where deepest strikes her kindly root
For hope or joy, for flower or fruit,
Least knows its happy part.

God only, and good angels, look
Behind the blissful screen '
As when, triumphant o'er His woes,
The Son of God by moonlight rose,
By all but Heaven unseen:

As when the holy Maid beheld
Her risen Son and Lord:
Thought has not colours half so fair
That she to paint that hour may dare,
In silence best ador'd.

The gracious Dove, that brought from Heaven
The earnest of our bliss,
Of many a chosen witness telling,
On many a happy vision dwelling,

THE CHRISTIAN YEAR

Sings not a note of this.

So, truest image of the Christ,
Old Israel's long-lost son,
What time, with sweet forgiving cheer,
He call'd his conscious brethren near,
Would weep with them alone.

He could not trust his melting soul
But in his Maker's sight '
Then why should gentle hearts and true
Bare to the rude world's withering view
Their treasure of delight!

No - let the dainty rose awhile
Her bashful fragrance hide '
Rend not her silken veil too soon,
But leave her, in her own soft noon,
To flourish and abide.

FIFTH SUNDAY IN LENT

And Moses said, I will now turn aside, and see this great sight,
why the bush is not burnt. Exodus iii. 3.

Th'historic Muse, from age to age,
Through many a waste heart-sickening page
Hath trac'd the works of Man:
But a celestial call to-day
Stays her, like Moses, on her way,
The works of God to scan.

Far seen across the sandy wild,
Where, like a solitary child,
He thoughtless roam'd and free,
One towering [47] thorn was wrapt in flame '
Bright without blaze it went and came:
Who would not turn and see?

Along the mountain ledges green
The scatter'd sheep at will may glean
The Desert's spicy stores:
The while, with undivided heart,
The shepherd talks with God apart,
And, as he talks, adores.

Ye too, who tend Christ's wildering flock,
Well may ye gather round the rock
That once was Sion's hill:

To watch the fire upon the mount
Still blazing, like the solar fount,
Yet unconsuming still.

Caught from that blaze by wrath Divine,
Lost branches of the once-loved vine,
Now wither'd, spent, and sere,
See Israel's sons, like glowing brands,
Tost wildly o'er a thousand lands
For twice a thousand year.

God will not quench nor slay them quite,
But lifts them like a beacon-light
The apostate Church to scare;
Or like pale ghosts that darkling roam,
Hovering around their ancient home,
But find no refuge there.

Ye blessed Angels! if of you
There be, who love the ways to view
Of Kings and Kingdoms here;
(And sure, 'tis worth an Angel's gaze,
To see, throughout that dreary maze,
God teaching love and fear:)

Oh say, in all the bleak expanse
Is there a spot to win your glance,
So bright, so dark as this?
A hopeless faith, a homeless race,
Yet seeking the most holy place,
And owning the true bliss!

Salted with fire they seem, [48] to show
How spirits lost in endless woe
May undecaying live.
Oh, sickening thought! yet hold it fast
Long as this glittering world shall last,

Or sin at heart survive.

And hark! amid the flashing fire,
Mingling with tones of fear and ire,
Soft Mercy's undersong '
'Tis Abraham's God who speaks so loud,
His people's cries have pierc'd the cloud,
He sees, He sees their wrong; [49]

He is come down to break their chain;
Though nevermore on Sion's fane
His visible ensign wave;
'Tis Sion, wheresoe'er they dwell,
Who, with His own true Israel,
Shall own Him strong to save.

He shall redeem them one by one,
Where'er the world-encircling sun
Shall see them meekly kneel:
All that He asks on Israel's part,
Is only that the captive heart
Its woe and burthen feel.

Gentiles! with fix'd yet awful eye
Turn ye this page of mystery,
Nor slight the warning sound:
'Put off thy shoes from off thy feet '
The place where man his God shall meet,
Be sure, is holy ground.'

[47] 'Seneth' said to be a sort of Acacia.
[48] St. Mark ix. 49.
[49] Exodus iii. 7, 8.

PALM SUNDAY

And He answered and said unto them, I tell you that, if these should hold their peace, the stones would immediately cry out.
St. Luke xix. 40.

Ye whose hearts are beating high
With the pulse of Poesy,
Heirs of more than royal race,
Fram'd by Heaven's peculiar grace,
God's own work to do on earth,
(If the word be not too bold,)
Giving virtue a new birth,
And a life that ne'er grows old '

Sovereign masters of all hearts!
Know ye, who hath set your parts?
He who gave you breath to sing,
By whose strength ye sweep the string,
He hath chosen you, to lead
His Hosannas here below; -
Mount, and claim your glorious meed;
Linger not with sin and woe.

But if ye should hold your peace,
Deem not that the song would cease '
Angels round His glory-throne,
Stars, His guiding hand that own,

Flowers, that grow beneath our feet,
Stones in earth's dark womb that rest,
High and low in choir shall meet,
Ere His Name shall be unblest.

Lord, by every minstrel tongue
Be Thy praise so duly sung,
That Thine angels'harps may ne'er
Fail to find fit echoing here:
We the while, of meaner birth,
Who in that divinest spell
Dare not hope to join on earth,
Give us grace to listen well.

But should thankless silence seal
Lips that might half Heaven reveal,
Should bards in idol-hymns profane
The sacred soul-enthralling strain,
(As in this bad world below
Noblest things find vilest using,)
Then, Thy power and mercy show,
In vile things noble breath infusing;

Then waken into sound divine
The very pavement of Thy shrine,
Till we, like Heaven's star-sprinkled floor,
Faintly give back what we adore:
Childlike though the voices be,
And untunable the parts,
Thou wilt own the minstrelsy
If it flow from childlike hearts.

MONDAY BEFORE EASTER

Doubtless Thou art our Father, though Abraham be ignorant of us, and Israel acknowledge us not. Isaiah lxiii. 16.

'Father to me thou art and mother dear,
And brother too, kind husband of my heart '
So speaks Andromache [50] in boding fear,
Ere from her last embrace her hero part '
So evermore, by Faith's undying glow,
We own the Crucified in weal or woe.

Strange to our ears the church-bells of our home,
This fragrance of our old paternal fields
May be forgotten; and the time may come
When the babe's kiss no sense of pleasure yields
E'en to the doting mother: but Thine own
Thou never canst forget, nor leave alone.

There are who sigh that no fond heart is theirs,
None loves them best - O vain and selfish sigh!
Out of the bosom of His love He spares '
The Father spares the Son, for thee to die:
For thee He died - for thee He lives again:
O'er thee He watches in His boundless reign.

Thou art as much His care, as if beside
Nor man nor angel liv'd in Heaven or earth:

KEBLE

Thus sunbeams pour alike their glorious tide
To light up worlds, or wake an insect's mirth:
They shine and shine with unexhausted store '
Thou art thy Saviour's darling - seek no more.

On thee and thine, thy warfare and thine end,
E'en in His hour of agony He thought,
When, ere the final pang His soul should rend,
The ransom'd spirits one by one were brought
To His mind's eye - two silent nights and days [51]
In calmness for His far-seen hour He stays.

Ye vaulted cells, where martyr'd seers of old
Far in the rocky walls of Sion sleep,
Green terraces and arched fountains cold,
Where lies the cypress shade so still and deep,
Dear sacred haunts of glory and of woe,
Help us, one hour, to trace His musings high and low:

One heart-ennobling hour! It may not be:
Th'unearthly thoughts have pass'd from earth away,
And fast as evening sunbeams from the sea
Thy footsteps all in Sion's deep decay
Were blotted from the holy ground: yet dear
Is every stone of hers; for Thou want surely here.

There is a spot within this sacred dale
That felt Thee kneeling - touch'd Thy prostrate brow:
One Angel knows it. O might prayer avail
To win that knowledge! sure each holy vow
Less quickly from the unstable soul would fade,
Offer'd where Christ in agony was laid.

Might tear of ours once mingle with the blood
That from His aching brow by moonlight fell,
Over the mournful joy our thoughts would brood,
Till they had fram'd within a guardian spell

100

To chase repining fancies, as they rise,
Like birds of evil wing, to mar our sacrifice.

So dreams the heart self-flattering, fondly dreams; -
Else wherefore, when the bitter waves o'erflow,
Miss we the light, Gethsemane, that streams
From thy dear name, where in His page of woe
It shines, a pale kind star in winter's sky?
Who vainly reads it there, in vain had seen Him die.

[50] Illiad, vi. 429.

[51] In Passion week, from Tuesday evening to Thursday evening; during which time Scripture seems to be nearly silent concernng our Saviour's proceedings.

TUESDAY BEFORE EASTER

They gave Him to drink wine mingled with myrrh: but He received in not. St.Mark xv. 23.

'Fill high the bowl, and spice it well, and pour
The dews oblivious: for the Cross is sharp,
The Cross is sharp, and He
Is tenderer than a lamb.

'He wept by Lazarus'grave - how will He bear
This bed of anguish? and His pale weak form
Is worn with many a watch
Of sorrow and unrest.

'His sweat last night was as great drops of blood,
And the sad burthen press'd Him so to earth,
The very torturers paus'd
To help Him on His way.

'Fill high the bowl, benumb His aching sense
With medicin'd sleep.' - O awful in Thy woe!
The parching thirst of death
Is on Thee, and Thou triest

The slumb'rous potion bland, and wilt not drink:
Not sullen, nor in scorn, like haughty man
With suicidal hand
Putting his solace by:

But as at first Thine all-pervading look
Saw from Thy Father's bosom to the abyss
Measuring in calm presage
The infinite descent;

So to the end, though now of mortal pangs
Made heir, and emptied of Thy glory, awhile,
With unaverted eye
Thou meetest all the storm.

Thou wilt feel all, that Thou mayst pity all;
And rather wouldst Thou wreathe with strong pain,
Than overcloud Thy soul,
So clear in agony,

Or lose one glimpse of Heaven before the time
O most entire and perfect sacrifice,
Renew'd in every pulse
That on the tedious Cross

Told the long hours of death, as, one by one,
The life-strings of that tender heart gave way;
E'en sinners, taught by Thee,
Look Sorrow in the face,

And bid her freely welcome, unbeguil'd
By false kind solaces, and spells of earth: '
And yet not all unsooth'd;
For when was Joy so dear,

As the deep calm that breath'd, 'Father, forgive,'
Or, 'Be with Me in Paradise to-day?'
And, though the strife be sore,
Yet in His parting breath

Love masters Agony; the soul that seem'd

Forsaken, feels her present God again,
And in her Father's arms
Contented dies away.

WEDNESDAY BEFORE EASTER

Saying, Father, if Thou be willing, remove this cup from Me;
nevertheless not My will, but Thine, be done. St. Luke xxii. 42.

O Lord my God, do thou Thy holy will '
I will lie still '
I will not stir, lest I forsake Thine arm,
And break the charm
Which lulls me, clinging to my Father's breast,
In perfect rest.

Wild fancy, peace! thou must not me beguile
With thy false smile:
I know thy flatteries and thy cheating ways;
Be silent, Praise,
Blind guide with siren voice, and blinding all
That hear thy call.

Come, Self-devotion, high and pure,
Thoughts that in thankfulness endure,
Though dearest hopes are faithless found,
And dearest hearts are bursting round.
Come, Resignation, spirit meek,
And let me kiss thy placid cheek,
And read in thy pale eye serene
Their blessing, who by faith can wean
Their hearts from sense, and learn to love

God only, and the joys above.

They say, who know the life divine,
And upward gaze with eagle eyne,
That by each golden crown on high, [52]
Rich with celestial jewelry,
Which for our Lord's redeemed is set,
There hangs a radiant coronet,
All gemmed with pure and living light,
Too dazzling for a sinner's sight,
Prepared for virgin souls, and them
Who seek the martyr's diadem.

Nor deem, who to that bliss aspire,
Must win their way through blood and fire.
The writhings of a wounded heart
Are fiercer than a foeman's dart.
Oft in Life's stillest shade reclining,
In Desolation unrepining,
Without a hope on earth to find
A mirror in an answering mind,
Meek souls there are, who little dream
Their daily strife an Angel's theme,
Or that the rod they take so calm
Shall prove in Heaven a martyr's palm.

And there are souls that seem to dwell
Above this earth - so rich a spell
Floats round their steps, where'er they move,
From hopes fulfilled and mutual love.
Such, if on high their thoughts are set,
Nor in the stream the source forget,
If prompt to quit the bliss they know,
Following the Lamb where'er He go,
By purest pleasures unbeguiled
To idolise or wife or child;
Such wedded souls our God shall own

For faultless virgins round His throne.

Thus everywhere we find our suffering God,
And where He trod
May set our steps: the Cross on Calvary
Uplifted high
Beams on the martyr host, a beacon light
In open fight.

To the still wrestlings of the lonely heart
He doth impart
The virtue of his midnight agony,
When none was nigh,
Save God and one good angel, to assuage
The tempest's rage.

Mortal! if life smile on thee, and thou find
All to thy mind,
Think, who did once from Heaven to Hell descend,
Thee to befriend:
So shalt thou dare forego, at His dear call,
Thy best, thine all.

'O Father! not My will, but Thine be done' '
So spake the Son.
Be this our charm, mellowing Earth's ruder noise
Of griefs and joys:
That we may cling for ever to Thy breast
In perfect rest!

[52] . . . .'that little coronet or special reward which God hath pre-
pared (extraordinary and besides the great Crown of all faithful
souls) for thos 'who have not defiled themselves with women,
but follow the (virgin) Lamb for ever.'' Bp. Taylor, Holy Living,
c. xi. sect. 3

THURSDAY BEFORE EASTER

As the beginning of thy supplications the commandment came
forth, and I am come to shew thee; for thou art greatly beloved:
therefore understand the matter, and consider the vision.
Daniel ix. 23.

'O Holy mountain of my God,
How do thy towers in ruin lie,
How art thou riven and strewn abroad,
Under the rude and wasteful sky!'
'Twas thus upon his fasting-day
The 'Man of Loves' was fain to pray,
His lattice [53] open toward his darling west,
Mourning the ruin'd home he still must love the best.

Oh! for a love like Daniel's now,
To wing to Heaven but one strong prayer
For God'S new Israel, sunk as low,
Yet flourishing to sight as fair,
As Sion in her height of pride,
With queens for handmaids at her side,
With kings her nursing-fathers, throned high,
And compass'd with the world's too tempting blazonry.

'Tis true, nor winter stays thy growth,
Nor torrid summer's sickly smile;
The flashing billows of the south

THE CHRISTIAN YEAR

Break not upon so lone an isle,
But thou, rich vine, art grafted there,
The fruit of death or life to bear,
Yielding a surer witness every day,
To thine Almighty Author and His steadfast sway.

Oh! grief to think, that grapes of gall
Should cluster round thine healthiest shoot!
God's herald prove a heartless thrall,
Who, if he dar'd, would fain be mute!
E'en such is this bad world we see,
Which self-condemned in owning Thee,
Yet dares not open farewell of Thee take,
For very pride, and her high-boasted Reason's sake.

What do we then? if far and wide
Men kneel to Christ, the pure and meek,
Yet rage with passion, swell with pride,
Have we not still our faith to seek?
Nay - but in steadfast humbleness
Kneel on to Him, who loves to bless
The prayer that waits for him; and trembling strive
To keep the lingering flame in thine own breast alive.

Dark frown'd the future e'en on him,
The loving and beloved Seer,
What time he saw, through shadows dim,
The boundary of th'eternal year;
He only of the sons of men
Nam'd to be heir of glory then. [54]
Else had it bruis'd too sore his tender heart
To see God'S ransom'd world in wrath and flame depart

Then look no more: or closer watch
Thy course in Earth's bewildering ways,
For every glimpse thine eye can catch
Of what shall be in those dread days:

So when th'Archangel's word is spoken,
And Death's deep trance for ever broken,
In mercy thou mayst feel the heavenly hand,
And in thy lot unharm'd before thy Savour stand. [55]

[53] Daniel vi. 10.
[54] Daniel xii. 13. See Bp. Kenn's Sermon on the character of Daniel.
[55] Thou shalt rest, and stand in thy lot at the end of days. Daniel xii.13.

GOOD FRIDAY

He is despised and rejected of men. Isaiah liii. 3.

Is it not strange, the darkest hour
That ever dawn'd on sinful earth
Should touch the heart with softer power
For comfort than an angel's mirth?
That to the Cross the mourner's eye should turn
Sooner than where the stars of Christmas burn?

Sooner than where the Easter sun
Shines glorious on yon open grave,
And to and fro the tidings run,
'Who died to heal, is risen to save?'
Sooner than where upon the Saviour's friends
The very Comforter in light and love descends?

Yet so it is: for duly there
The bitter herbs of earth are set,
Till temper'd by the Saviour's prayer,
And with the Saviour's life-blood wet,
They turn to sweetness, and drop holy balm,
Soft as imprison'd martyr's deathbed calm.

All turn to sweet - but most of all
That bitterest to the lip of pride,
When hopes presumptuous fade and fall,
Or Friendship scorns us, duly tried,

Or Love, the flower that closes up for fear
When rude and selfish spirits breathe too near.

Then like a long-forgotten strain
Comes sweeping o'er the heart forlorn
What sunshine hours had taught in vain
Of Jesus suffering shame and scorn,
As in all lowly hearts he suffers still,
While we triumphant ride and have the world at will.

His pierced hands in vain would hide
His face from rude reproachful gaze,
His ears are open to abide
The wildest storm the tongue can raise,
He who with one rough word, [56] some early day,
Their idol world and them shall sweep for aye away.

But we by Fancy may assuage
The festering sore by Fancy made,
Down in some lonely hermitage
Like wounded pilgrims safely laid,
Where gentlest breezes whisper souls distress'd,
That Love yet lives, and Patience shall find rest.

O! shame beyond the bitterest thought
That evil spirit ever fram'd,
That sinners know what Jesus wrought,
Yet feel their haughty hearts untam'd '
That souls in refuge, holding by the Cross,
Should wince and fret at this world's little loss.

Lord of my heart, by Thy last cry,
Let not Thy blood on earth be spent '
Lo, at Thy feet I fainting lie,
Mine eyes upon Thy wounds are bent,
Upon Thy streaming wounds my weary eyes
Wait like the parched earth on April skies.

Wash me, and dry these bitter tears,
O let my heart no further roam,
'Tis Thine by vows, and hopes, and fears.
Long since - O call Thy wanderer home;
To that dear home, safe in Thy wounded side,
Where only broken hearts their sin and shame may hide.

[56] Wisdom of Solomon, xii. 9.

EASTER EVE

As for thee also, by the blood of thy covenant I have sent forth
thy prisoners out of the pit wherein is no water. Zechariah ix. 11.

At length the worst is o'er, and Thou art laid
Deep in Thy darksome bed;
All still and cold beneath yon dreary stone
Thy sacred form is gone;
Around those lips where power and mercy hung,
The dews of deaths have clung;
The dull earth o'er Thee, and Thy foes around,
Thou sleep'st a silent corse, in funeral fetters wound.

Sleep'st Thou indeed? or is Thy spirit fled,
At large among the dead?
Whether in Eden bowers Thy welcome voice
Wake Abraham to rejoice,
Or in some drearier scene Thine eye controls
The thronging band of souls;
That, as Thy blood won earth, Thine agony
Might set the shadowy realm from sin and sorrow free.

Where'er Thou roam'st, one happy soul, we know,
Seen at Thy side in woe, [57]
Waits on Thy triumphs - even as all the blest
With him and Thee shall rest.
Each on his cross; by Thee we hang a while,
Watching Thy patient smile,

Till we have learn'd to say, "'Tis justly done,
Only in glory, Lord, Thy sinful servant own.'

Soon wilt Thou take us to Thy tranquil bower
To rest one little hour,
Till Thine elect are number'd, and the grave
Call Thee to come and save:
Then on Thy bosom borne shall we descend
Again with earth to blend,
Earth all refin'd with bright supernal fires,
Tinctur'd with holy blood, and wing'd with pure desires.

Meanwhile with every son and saint of Thine
Along the glorious line,
Sitting by turns beneath Thy sacred feet
We'll hold communion sweet,
Know them by look and voice, and thank them all
For helping us in thrall,
For words of hope, and bright examples given
To show through moonless skies that there is light in Heaven.

O come that day, when in this restless heart
Earth shall resign her part,
When in the grave with Thee my limbs shall rest,
My soul with Thee be blest!
But stay, presumptuous - Christ with Thee abides
In the rock's dreary sides:
He from this stone will wring Celestial dew
If but this prisoner's heart he faithful found and true.

When tears are spent, and then art left alone
With ghosts of blessings gone,
Think thou art taken from the cross, and laid
In Jesus' burial shade;
Take Moses' rod, the rod of prayer, and call
Out of the rocky wall
The fount of holy blood; and lift on high

Thy grovelling soul that feels so desolate and dry.

Prisoner of hope thou art [58] - look up and sing
In hope of promis'd spring.
As in the pit his father's darling lay [59]
Beside the desert way,
And knew not how, but knew his GOD would save
E'en from that living grave,
So, buried with our Lord, we'll chose our eyes
To the decaying world, till Angels bid us rise.

[57] St. Luke xxiii. 43.

[58] Turn ye to the stronghold, ye prisoners of hope. Zechariah ix. 12.

[59] They took him, and cast him into a pit: and the pit was empty, there was no water in it. Genesis xxxvii. 24.

EASTER DAY

And as they were afraid, and bowed down their faces to the earth, they said unto them, Why seek ye the living among the dead? He is not here, but is risen. St. Luke xxiv. 5, 6.

Oh! day of days! shall hearts set free
No 'minstrel rapture' find for thee?
Thou art this Sun of other days,
They shine by giving back thy rays:

Enthroned in thy sovereign sphere,
Thou shedd'st thy light on all the year;
Sundays by thee more glorious break,
An Easter Day in every week:

And week days, following in their train,
The fulness of thy blessing gain,
Till all, both resting soil employ,
Be one Lord's day of holy joy.

Then wake, my soul, to high desires,
And earlier light thine altar fires:
The World some hours is on her way,
Nor thinks on thee, thou blessed day:

Or, if she think, it is in scorn:
The vernal light of Easter morn
To her dark gaze no brighter seems

Than Reason's or the Law's pale beams.

'Where is your Lord?' she scornful asks:
'Where is His hire? we know his tasks;
Sons of a King ye boast to be:
Let us your crowns and treasures see.'

We in the words of Truth reply,
(An angel brought them from this sky,)
'Our crown, our treasure is not here,
'Tis stor'd above the highest sphere:

'Methinks your wisdom guides amiss,
To seek on earth a Christian's bliss;
We watch not now the lifeless stone;
Our only Lord is risen and gone.'

Yet e'en the lifeless stone is dear
For thoughts of Him who late lay here;
And the base world, now Christ hath died,
Ennobled is and glorified.

No more a charnel-house, to fence
The relics of lost innocence,
A vault of ruin and decay;
Th' imprisoning stone is roll'd away:

'Tis now a cell, where angels use
To come and go with heavenly news,
And in the ears of mourners say,
'Come, see the place where Jesus lay:'

'Tis now a fane, where Love can find
Christ everywhere embalm'd and shin'd:
Aye gathering up memorials sweet,
Where'er she sets her duteous feet.

Oh! joy to Mary first allow'd,
When rous'd from weeping o'er His shroud,
By His own calm, soul-soothing tone,
Breathing her name, as still His own!

Joy to the faithful Three renew'd,
As their glad errand they pursued!
Happy, who so Christ's word convey,
That he may meet them on their way!

So is it still: to holy tears,
In lonely hours, Christ risen appears:
In social hours, who Christ would see
Must turn all tasks to Charity.

MONDAY IN EASTER WEEK

Of a truth I perceive that God is no respecter of persons: but in every nation he that feareth Him, and worketh righteousness, is accepted with Him. Acts x. 34, 35.

Go up and watch the new-born rill
Just trickling from its mossy bed,
Streaking the heath-clad hill
With a bright emerald thread.

Canst thou her bold career foretell,
What rocks she shall o'erleap or rend,
How far in Ocean's swell
Her freshening billows send?

Perchance that little brook shall flow
The bulwark of some mighty realm,
Bear navies to and fro
With monarchs at their helm.

Or canst thou guess, how far away
Some sister nymph, beside her urn
Reclining night and day,
'Mid reeds and mountain fern,

Nurses her store, with thine to blend
When many a moor and glen are past,

Then in the wide sea end
Their spotless lives at last?

E'en so, the course of prayer who knows?
It springs in silence where it will,
Springs out of sight, and flows
At first a lonely rill:

But streams shall meet it by and by
From thousand sympathetic hearts,
Together swelling high
Their chant of many parts.

Unheard by all but angel ears
The good Cornelius knelt alone,
Nor dream'd his prayers and tears
Would help a world undone.

The while upon his terrac'd roof
The lov'd Apostle to his Lord
In silent thought aloof
For heavenly vision soar'd.

Far o'er the glowing western main
His wistful brow was upward rais'd,
Where, like an angel's train,
The burnish'd water blaz'd.

The saint beside the ocean pray'd,
This soldier in his chosen bower,
Where all his eye survey'd
Seem'd sacred in that hour.

To each unknown his brother's prayer,
Yet brethren true in dearest love
Were they - and now they share
Fraternal joys above.

There daily through Christ's open gate
They see the Gentile spirits press,
Brightening their high estate
With dearer happiness.

What civic wreath for comrades sav'd
Shone ever with such deathless gleam,
Or when did perils brav'd
So sweet to veterans seem?

TUESDAY IN EASTER WEEK

And they departed quickly from the sepulchre with fear and great joy, and did run to bring His disciples word.
St. Matthew xxviii. 8.

TO THE SNOWDROP.

Thou first-born of the year's delight,
Pride of the dewy glade,
In vernal green and virgin white,
Thy vestal robes, array'd:

'Tis not because thy drooping form
Sinks graceful on its nest,
When chilly shades from gathering storm
Affright thy tender breast;

Nor for yon river islet wild
Beneath the willow spray,
Where, like the ringlets of a child,
Thou weav'st thy circle gay;

'Tis not for these I love thee dear '
Thy shy averted smiles
To Fancy bode a joyous year,
One of Life's fairy isles.

They twinkle to the wintry moon,
And cheer th' ungenial day,
And tell us, all will glisten soon
As green and bright as they.

Is there a heart that loves the spring,
Their witness can refuse?
Yet mortals doubt, when angels bring
From Heaven their Easter news:

When holy maids and matrons speak
Of Christ's forsaken bed,
And voices, that forbid to seek
The hiving 'mid the dead,

And when they say, 'Turn, wandering heart,
Thy Lord is ris'n indeed,
Let Pleasure go, put Care apart,
And to His presence speed;'

We smile in scorn: and yet we know
They early sought the tomb,
Their hearts, that now so freshly glow,
Lost in desponding gloom.

They who have sought, nor hope to find,
Wear not so bright a glance:
They, who have won their earthly mind,
Lees reverently advance.

But where in gentle spirits, fear
And joy so duly meet,
These sure have seen the angels near,
And kiss'd the Saviour's feet.

Nor let the Pastor's thankful eye
Their faltering tale disdain,

THE CHRISTIAN YEAR

As on their lowly couch they lie,
Prisoners of want and pain.

O guide us, when our faithless hearts
From Thee would start aloof,
Where Patience her sweet skill imparts
Beneath some cottage roof:

Revive our dying fires, to burn
High as her anthems soar,
And of our scholars let us learn
Our own forgotten lore.

FIRST SUNDAY AFTER EASTER

Seemeth it but a small thing unto you, that the God of Israel hath
separated you from the congregation of Israel, to bring you near
to Himself? Numbers xvi. 9.

First Father of the holy seed,
If yet, invok'd in hour of need,
Thou count me for Thine own
Not quite an outcast if I prove,
(Thou joy'st in miracles of love),
Hear, from Thy mercy-throne!

Upon Thine altar's horn of gold
Help me to lay my trembling hold,
Though stain'd with Christian gore; -
The blood of souls by Thee redeem'd,
But, while I rov'd or idly dream'd,
Lost to be found no more.

For oft, when summer leaves were bright,
And every flower was bath'd in light,
In sunshine moments past,
My wilful heart would burst away
From where the holy shadow lay,
Where heaven my lot had cast.

I thought it scorn with Thee to dwell,
A Hermit in a silent cell,

While, gaily sweeping by,
Wild Fancy blew his bugle strain,
And marshall'd all his gallant train
In the world's wondering eye.

I would have join'd him - but as oft
Thy whisper'd warnings, kind and soft,
My better soul confess'd.
'My servant, let the world alone '
Safe on the steps of Jesus' throne
Be tranquil and be blest.'

'Seems it to thee a niggard hand
That nearest Heaven has bade thee stand,
The ark to touch and bear,
With incense of pure heart's desire
To heap the censer's sacred fire,
The snow-white Ephod wear?'

Why should we crave the worldling's wreath,
On whom the Savour deign'd to breathe,
To whom His keys were given,
Who lead the choir where angels meet,
With angels' food our brethren greet,
And pour the drink of Heaven?

When sorrow all our heart would ask,
We need not shun our daily task,
And hide ourselves for calm;
The herbs we seek to heal our woe
Familiar by our pathway grow,
Our common air is balm.

Around each pure domestic shrine
Bright flowers of Eden bloom and twine,
Our hearths are altars all;
The prayers of hungry souls and poor,

Like armed angels at the door,
Our unseen foes appal.

Alms all around and hymns within '
What evil eye can entrance win
Where guards like these abound?
If chance some heedless heart should roam,
Sure, thought of these will lure it home
Ere lost in Folly's round.

O joys, that sweetest in decay,
Fall not, like wither'd leaves, away,
But with the silent breath
Of violets drooping one by one,
Soon as their fragrant task is done,
Are wafted high in death!

SECOND SUNDAY AFTER EASTER

He hath said, which heard the words of God, and knew the
knowledge of the Most High, which saw the vision of the Al-
mighty, falling into a trance, but having his eyes open: I shall see
Him, but not now; I shall behold Him, but not nigh; there shall
come a Star out at Jacob, and a Sceptre shall rise out of Israel,
and shall smite the corners of Moab, and destroy all the children
at Sheth. Numbers xxiv. 16, 17.

O for a sculptor's hand,
That thou might'st take thy stand,
Thy wild hair floating on the eastern breeze,
Thy tranc'd yet open gaze
Fix'd on the desert haze,
As one who deep in heaven some airy pageant sees.

In outline dim and vast
Their fearful shadows cast
This giant forms of empires on their way
To ruin: one by one
They tower and they are gone,
Yet in the Prophet's soul the dreams of avarice stay.

No sun or star so bright
In all the world of light
That they should draw to Heaven his downward eye:
He hears th' Almighty's word,

KEBLE

He sees the angel's sword,
Yet low upon the earth his heart and treasure lie.

Lo! from you argent field,
To him and us reveal'd,
One gentle Star glides down, on earth to dwell.
Chain'd as they are below
Our eyes may see it glow,
And as it mounts again, may track its brightness well.

To him it glar'd afar,
A token of wild war,
The banner of his Lord's victorious wrath:
But close to us it gleams,
Its soothing lustre streams
Around our home's green walls, and on our church-way path.

We in the tents abide
Which he at distance eyed
Like goodly cedars by the waters spread,
While seven red altar-fires
Rose up in wavy spires,
Where on the mount he watch'd his sorceries dark and dread.

He watch'd till morning's ray
On lake and meadow lay,
And willow-shaded streams that silent sweep
Around the banner'd lines,
Where by their several signs
The desert-wearied tribes in sight of Canaan sleep.

He watch'd till knowledge came
Upon his soul like flame,
Not of those magic fires at random caught:
But true Prophetic light
Flash'd o'er him, high and bright,
Flash'd once, and died away, and left his darken'd thought.

And can he choose but fear,
Who feels his God so near,
That when he fain would curse, his powerless tongue
In blessing only moves? '
Alas! the world he loves
Too close around his heart her tangling veil hath flung.

Sceptre and Star divine,
Who in Thine inmost shrine
Hash made us worshippers, O claim Thine own;
More than Thy seers we know '
O teach our love to grow
Up to Thy heavenly light, and reap what Thou hast sown.

THIRD SUNDAY AFTER EASTER

A woman when she is in travail hath sorrow, because her hour is come; but as soon as she is delivered of the child, she remembereth no more the anguish, for joy that a man is born into the world. St. John xvi. 21.

Well may I guess and feel
Why Autumn should be sad;
But vernal airs should sorrow heal,
Spring should be gay and glad:
Yet as along this violet bank I rove,
The languid sweetness seems to choke my breath,
I sit me down beside the hazel grove,
And sigh, and half could wish my weariness were death.

Like a bright veering cloud
Grey blossoms twinkle there,
Warbles around a busy crowd
Of larks in purest air.
Shame on the heart that dreams of blessings gone,
Or wakes the spectral forms of woe and crime,
When nature sings of joy and hope alone,
Reading her cheerful lesson in her own sweet time.

Nor let the proud heart say,
In her self-torturing hour,
The travail pangs must have their way,
The aching brow must lower.

THE CHRISTIAN YEAR

To us long since the glorious Child is born
Our throes should be forgot, or only seem
Like a sad vision told for joy at morn,
For joy that we have wak'd and found it but a dream.

Mysterious to all thought
A mother's prime of bliss,
When to her eager lips is brought
Her infant's thrilling kiss.
O never shall it set, the sacred light
Which dawns that moment on her tender gaze,
In the eternal distance blending bright
Her darling's hope and hers, for love and joy and praise.

No need for her to weep
Like Thracian wives of yore,
Save when in rapture still and deep
Her thankful heart runs o'er.
They mourn'd to trust their treasure on the main,
Sure of the storm, unknowing of their guide:
Welcome to her the peril and the pain,
For well she knows the bonus where they may safely hide.

She joys that one is born
Into a world forgiven,
Her Father's household to adorn,
And dwell with her in Heaven.
So have I seen, in Spring's bewitching hour,
When the glad Earth is offering all her best,
Some gentle maid bend o'er a cherish'd flower,
And wish it worthier on a Parent's heart to rest.

FOURTH SUNDAY AFTER EASTER

Nevertheless I tell you the truth; It is expedient for you that I go away: for if I go not away, the Comforter will not come unto you; but if I depart, I will send Him unto you. St. John xvi. 7.

My Saviour, can it ever be
That I should gain by losing Thee?
The watchful mother tarries nigh,
Though sleep have closed her infant's eye;
For should he wake, and find her gone.
She knows she could not bear his moan.
But I am weaker than a child,
And Thou art more than mother dear;
Without Thee Heaven were but a wild;
How can I live without Thee here!

''Tis good for you, that I should go,
You lingering yet awhile below;' '
'Tis Thine own gracious promise, Lord!
Thy saints have prov'd the faithful word,
When heaven's bright boundless avenue
Far open'd on their eager view,
And homeward to Thy Father's throne,
Still lessening, brightening on their sight,
Thy shadowy car went soaring on;
They track'd Thee up th' abyss of light.

Thou bidd'st rejoice; they dare not mourn,
But to their home in gladness turn,
Their home and God's, that favour'd place,
Where still He shines on Abraham's race,
In prayers and blessings there to wait
Like suppliants at their Monarch's gate,
Who bent with bounty rare to aid
The splendours of His crowning day,
Keeps back awhile His largess, made
More welcome for that brief delay:

In doubt they wait, but not unblest;
They doubt not of their Master's rest,
Nor of the gracious will of Heaven '
Who gave His Son, sure all has given '
But in ecstatic awe they muse
What course the genial stream may choose,
And far and wide their fancies rove,
And to their height of wonder strain,
What secret miracle of love
Should make their Saviour's going gain.

The days of hope and prayer are past,
The day of comfort dawns at last,
The everlasting gates again
Roll back, and, lo! a royal train '
From the far depth of light once more
The floods of glory earthward pour:
They part like shower-drops in mid air,
But ne'er so soft fell noon-tide shower,
Nor ev'ning rainbow gleam'd so fair
To weary swains in parched bower.

Swiftly and straight each tongue of flame
Through cloud and breeze unwavering came,
And darted to its place of rest

On some meek brow of Jesus blest.
Nor fades it yet, that living gleam,
And still those lambent lightnings stream;
Where'er the Lord is, there are they;
In every heart that gives them room,
They light His altar every day,
Zeal to inflame, and vice consume.

Soft as the plumes of Jesus' Dove
They nurse the soul to heavenly love;
The struggling spark of good within,
Just smother'd in the strife of sin,
They quicken to a timely glow,
The pure flame spreading high and low.
Said I, that prayer and hope were o'er?
Nay, blessed Spirit! but by Thee
The Church's prayer finds wings to soar,
The Church's hope finds eyes to see.

Then, fainting soul, arise and sing;
Mount, but be sober on the wing;
Mount up, for Heaven is won by prayer,
Be sober, for thou art not there;
Till Death the weary spirit free,
Thy God hath said, 'Tis good for thee
To walk by faith and not by sight:
Take it on trust a little while;
Soon shalt thou read the mystery right
In the full sunshine of His smile.

Or if thou yet more knowledge crave,
Ask thine own heart, that willing slave
To all that works thee woe or harm
Shouldst thou not need some mighty charm
To win thee to thy Saviour's side,
Though He had deign'd with thee to bide?
The Spirit must stir the darkling deep,

THE CHRISTIAN YEAR

The Dove must settle on the Cross,
Else we should all sin on or sleep
With Christ in sight, turning our gain to loss.

FIFTH SUNDAY AFTER EASTER

ROGATION SUNDAY

And the Lord was very angry with Aaron to have destroyed him:
and I prayed for Aaron also the same time. Deuteronomy ix. 20.

Now is there solemn pause in earth and heaven;
The Conqueror now
His bonds hath riven,
And Angels wonder why He stays below:
Yet hath not man his lesson learn'd,
How endless love should be return'd.

Deep is the silence as of summer noon,
When a soft shower
Will trickle soon,
A gracious rain, freshening the weary bower '
O sweetly then far off is heard
The clear note of some lonely bird.

So let Thy turtle-dove's sad call arise
In doubt and fear
Through darkening skies,
And pierce, O Lord, Thy justly-sealed ear,
Where on the house-top, [60] all night long
She trills her widow'd, faltering song.

Teach her to know and love her hour of prayer,
And evermore,
As faith grows rare,
Unlock her heart, and offer all its store
In holier love and humbler vows,
As suits a lost returning spouse.

Not as at first, [61] but with intenser cry,
Upon the mount
She now must lie,
Till Thy dear love to blot the sad account
Of her rebellious race be won,
Pitying the mother in the son.

But chiefly (for she knows Thee anger'd worst
By holiest things
Profan'd and curst),
Chiefly for Aaron's seed she spreads her wings,
If but one leaf she may from Thee
Win of the reconciling tree.

For what shall heal, when holy water banes!
Or who may guide
O'er desert plains
Thy lov'd yet sinful people wandering wide,
If Aaron's hand unshrinking mould [62]
An idol form of earthly gold?

Therefore her tears are bitter, and as deep
Her boding sigh,
As, while men sleep,
Sad-hearted mothers heave, that wakeful lie,
To muse upon some darling child
Roaming in youth's uncertain wild.

Therefore on fearful dreams her inward sight

Is fain to dwell '
What lurid light
Shall the last darkness of the world dispel,
The Mediator in His wrath
Descending down the lightning's path.

Yet, yet awhile, offended Saviour, pause,
In act to break [63]
Thine outrag'd laws,
O spare Thy rebels for Thine own dear sake;
Withdraw Thine hand, nor dash to earth
The covenant of our second birth.

'Tis forfeit like the first - we own it all '
Yet for love's sake
Let it not fall;
But at Thy touch let veiled hearts awake,
That nearest to Thine altar lie,
Yet least of holy things descry.

Teacher of teachers! Priest of priests! from Thee
The sweet strong prayer
Must rise, to free
First Levi, then all Israel, from the snare.
Thou art our Moses out of sight '
Speak for us, or we perish quite.

[60] Psalm cii. 7.
[61] I fell down before the Lord forty days and forty nights, as I
fell down at the first. Deuteronomy ix. 25.
[62] Exodus xxxii. 4.
[63] Exodus xxxii. 19.

ASCENSION DAY

Why stand ye gazing up into Heaven? this same Jesus, which is taken up from you into Heaven, shall so come in like manner as ye have seen Him go into Heaven. Acts i. 11.

Soft cloud, that while the breeze of May
Chants her glad matins in the leafy arch,
Draw'st thy bright veil across the heavenly way
Meet pavement for an angel's glorious march:

My soul is envious of mine eye,
That it should soar and glide with thee so fast,
The while my grovelling thoughts half buried lie,
Or lawless roam around this earthly waste.

Chains of my heart, avaunt I say '
I will arise, and in the strength of love
Pursue the bright track ere it fade away,
My Saviour's pathway to His home above.

Sure, when I reach the point where earth
Melts into nothing from th' uncumber'd sight,
Heaven will o'ercome th' attraction of my birth.
And I shall sink in yonder sea of light:

Till resting by th' incarnate Lord,
Once bleeding, now triumphant for my sake,
I mark Him, how by seraph hosts ador'd,

He to earth's lowest cares is still awake.

The sun and every vassal star,
All space, beyond the soar of angel wings,
Wait on His word: and yet He stays His car
For every sigh a contrite suppliant brings.

He listens to the silent tear
For all the anthems of the boundless sky '
And shall our dreams of music bar our ear
To His soul-piercing voice for ever nigh?

Nay, gracious Saviour - but as now
Our thoughts have trac'd Thee to Thy glory-throne
So help us evermore with thee to bow
Where human sorrow breathes her lowly moan.

We must not stand to gaze too long,
Though on unfolding Heaven our gaze we bend
Where lost behind the bright angelic throng
We see CHRIST'S entering triumph slow ascend.

No fear but we shall soon behold,
Faster than now it fades, that gleam revive,
When issuing from his cloud of fiery gold
Our wasted frames feel the true sun, and live.

Then shall we see Thee as Thou art,
For ever fix'd in no unfruitful gaze,
But such as lifts the new-created heart,
Age after age, in worthier love and praise.

SUNDAY AFTER ASCENSION

As every man hath received the gift, even so minister the same
one to another, as good stewards of the manifold grace of God.
1 St. Peter iv. 10.

The Earth that in her genial breast
Makes for the down a kindly nest,
Where wafted by the warm south-west
It floats at pleasure,
Yields, thankful, of her very best,
To nurse her treasure:

True to her trust, tree, herb, or reed,
She renders for each scatter'd seed,
And to her Lord with duteous heed
Gives large increase:
Thus year by year she works unfeed,
And will not cease.

Woe worth these barren hearts of ours,
Where Thou hast set celestial flowers,
And water'd with more balmy showers
Than e'er distill'd
In Eden, on th' ambrosial bowers '
Yet nought we yield.

Largely Thou givest, gracious Lord,
Largely Thy gifts should be restor'd;

Freely Thou givest, and Thy word
Is, 'Freely give.' [64]
He only, who forgets to hoard,
Has learn'd to live.

Wisely Thou givest - all around
Thine equal rays are resting found,
Yet varying so on various ground
They pierce and strike,
That not two roseate cups are crown'd
With drew alike:

E'en so, in silence, likest Thee,
Steals on soft-handed Charity,
Tempering her gifts, that seem so free,
By time and place,
Till not a woe the bleak world see,
But finds her grace:

Eyes to the blind, and to the lame
Feet, and to sinners wholesome blame,
To starving bodies food and flame,
By turns she brings;
To humbled souls, that sink for shame,
Lends heaven-ward wings:

Leads them the way our Saviour went,
And shows Love's treasure yet unspent;
As when th' unclouded heavens were rent.
Opening His road,
Nor yet His Holy Spirit sent
To our abode.

Ten days th' eternal doors display'd
Were wondering (so th' Almighty bade)
Whom Love enthron'd would send, in aid
Of souls that mourn,

Left orphans in Earth's dreary shade
As noon as born.

Open they stand, that prayers in throngs
May rise on high, and holy songs,
Such incense as of right belongs
To the true shrine,
Where stands the Healer of all wrongs
In light divine;

The golden censer in His hand,
He offers hearts from every land,
Tied to His own by gentlest band
Of silent Love:
About Him winged blessings stand
In act to move.

A little while, and they shall fleet
From Heaven to Earth, attendants meet
On the life-giving Paraclete
Speeding His flight,
With all that sacred is and sweet,
On saints to light.

Apostles, Prophets, Pastors, all
Shall feel the shower of Mercy fall,
And startling at th' Almighty's call,
Give what He gave,
Till their high deeds the world appal,
And sinners save.

[64] St. Matthew x. 8.

WHITSUNDAY

And suddenly there came a sound from Heaven as of a rushing
mighty wind, and it filled all the house where they were sitting.
And there appeared unto them cloven tongues like as of fire, and
it sat upon each of them. And they were all filled with the Holy
Ghost. Acts ii. 2-4.

When God of old came down from Heaven,
In power and wrath He came;
Before His feet the clouds were riven,
Half darkness and half flame:

Around the trembling mountain's base
The prostrate people lay;
A day of wrath and not of grace;
A dim and dreadful day.

But when he came the second time,
He came in power and love,
Softer than gale at morning prime
Hover'd His holy Dove.

The fires that rush'd on Sinai down
In sudden torrents dread,
Now gently light, a glorious crown,
On every sainted head.

Like arrows went those lightnings forth

Wing'd with the sinner's doom,
But these, like tongues, o'er all the earth
Proclaiming life to come:

And as on Israel's awe-struck ear
The voice exceeding loud,
The trump, that angels quake to hear,
Thrill'd from the deep, dark cloud;

So, when the Spirit of our God
Came down His flock to find,
A voice from Heaven was heard abroad,
A rushing, mighty wind.

Nor doth the outward ear alone
At that high warning start;
Conscience gives back th' appalling tone;
'Tis echoed in the heart.

It fills the Church of God; it fills
The sinful world around;
Only in stubborn hearts and wills
No place for it is found.

To other strains our souls are set:
A giddy whirl of sin
Fills ear and brain, and will not let
Heaven's harmonies come in.

Come Lord, Come Wisdom, Love, and Power,
Open our ears to hear;
Let us not miss th' accepted hour;
Save, Lord, by Love or Fear.

MONDAY IN WHITSUN-WEEK

So the Lord scattered them abroad from thence upon the face of
all the earth; and they left off to build the city. Genesis xi. 8.

Since all that is not Heaven must fade,
Light be the hand of Ruin laid
Upon the home I love:
With lulling spell let soft Decay
Steal on, and spare the giant sway,
The crash of tower and grove.

Far opening down some woodland deep
In their own quiet glade should sleep
The relics dear to thought,
And wild-flower wreaths from side to side
Their waving tracery hang, to hide
What ruthless Time has wrought.

Such are the visions green and sweet
That o'er the wistful fancy fleet
In Asia's sea-like plain,
Where slowly, round his isles of sand,
Euphrates through the lonely land
Winds toward the pearly main.

Slumber is there, but not of rest;
There her forlorn and weary nest
The famish'd hawk has found,

The wild dog howls at fall of night,
The serpent's rustling coils affright
The traveller on his round.

What shapeless form, half lost on high, [65]
Half seen against the evening sky,
Seems like a ghost to glide,
And watch, from Babel's crumbling heap,
Where in her shadow, fast asleep,
Lies fallen imperial Pride?

With half-clos'd eye a lion there
Is basking in his noontide lair,
Or prowls in twilight gloom.
The golden city's king he seems,
Such as in old prophetic dreams [66]
Sprang from rough ocean's womb.

But where are now his eagle wings,
That shelter'd erst a thousand kings,
Hiding the glorious sky
From half the nations, till they own
No holier name, no mightier throne?
That vision is gone by.

Quench'd is the golden statue's ray, [67]
The breath of heaven has blown away
What toiling earth had pil'd,
Scattering wise heart and crafty hand,
As breezes strew on ocean's sand
The fabrics of a child.

Divided thence through every age
Thy rebels, Lord, their warfare wage,
And hoarse and jarring all
Mount up their heaven-assailing cries
To Thy bright watchmen in the skies

From Babel's shatter'd wall.

Thrice only since, with blended might
The nations on that haughty height
Have met to scale the Heaven:
Thrice only might a Seraph's look
A moment's shade of sadness brook '
Such power to guilt was given.

Now the fierce bear and leopard keen [68]
Are perish'd as they ne'er had been,
Oblivion is their home:
Ambition's boldest dream and last
Must melt before the clarion blast
That sounds the dirge of Rome.

Heroes and kings, obey the charm,
Withdraw the proud high-reaching arm,
There is an oath on high:
That ne'er on brow of mortal birth
Shall blend again the crowns of earth,
Nor in according cry

Her many voices mingling own
One tyrant Lord, one idol throne:
But to His triumphs soon
HE shall descend, who rules above,
And the pure language of His love, [69]
All tongues of men shall tune.

Nor let Ambition heartless mourn;
When Babel's very ruins burn,
Her high desires may breathe; -
O'ercome thyself, and thou mayst share
With Christ His Father's throne, [70] and wear
The world's imperial wreath.

[65] See Sir R. K. Porter's Travels, ii. 387. 'In my second visit to Birs Nimrod, my party suddenly halted, having descried several dark objects moving along the summit of its hill, which they construed into dismounted Arabs on the lookout: I took out my glass to examine, and soon distinguished that the causes of our alarm were two or three majestic lions, taking the air upon the heights of the pyramid.'

[66] Daniel vii. 4.

[67] Daniel ii. and iii.

[68] Daniel vii. 5, 6.

[69] Then will I turn to the people a pure language, that they may all call upon the name of the Lord, to serve Him with one consent. Zephaniah iii. 9.

[70] To him that overcometh will I grant to sit with Me in My throne. Revelations iii. 21.

TUESDAY IN WHITSUN-WEEK

When He putteth forth His own sheep, He goeth before them. St.
John x. 4.

(Addressed to Candidates for Ordination.)

'Lord, in Thy field I work all day,
I read, I teach, I warn, I pray,
And yet these wilful wandering sheep
Within Thy fold I cannot keep.

'I journey, yet no step is won '
Alas! the weary course I run!
Like sailors shipwreck'd in their dreams,
All powerless and benighted seems.'

What? wearied out with half a life?
Scar'd with this smooth unbloody strife?
Think where thy coward hopes had flown
Had Heaven held out the martyr's crown.

How couldst thou hang upon the cross,
To whom a weary hour is loss?
Or how the thorns and scourging brook
Who shrinkest from a scornful look?

Yet ere thy craven spirit faints,
Hear thine own King, the King of Saints;

Though thou wert toiling in the grave,
'Tis He can cheer thee, He can save.

He is th' eternal mirror bright,
Where Angels view the FATHER'S light,
And yet in Him the simplest swain
May read his homely lesson plain.

Early to quit His home on earth,
And claim His high celestial birth,
Alone with His true Father found
Within the temple's solemn round: '

Yet in meek duty to abide
For many a year at Mary's side,
Nor heed, though restless spirits ask,
'What, hath the Christ forgot His task?'

Conscious of Deity within,
To bow before an heir of sin,
With folded arms on humble breast,
By His own servant wash'd and blest: '

Then full of Heaven, the mystic Dove
Hovering His gracious brow above,
To shun the voice and eye of praise,
And in the wild His trophies raise: '

With hymns of angels in His ears,
Back to His task of woe and tears,
Unmurmuring through the world to roam
With not a wish or thought at home: '

All but Himself to heal and save,
Till ripen'd for the cross and grave,
He to His Father gently yield
The breath that our redemption seal'd: '

Then to unearthly life arise,
Yet not at once to seek the skies,
But glide awhile from saint to saint,
Lest on our lonely way we faint;

And through the cloud by glimpses show
How bright, in Heaven, the marks will glow
Of the true cross, imprinted deep
Both on the Shepherd and the sheep: '

When out of sight, in heart and prayer,
Thy chosen people still to bear,
And from behind Thy glorious veil,
Shed light that cannot change or fail: '

This is Thy pastoral course, O Lord,
Till we be sav'd, and Thou ador'd; -
Thy course and ours - but who are they
Who follow on the narrow way?

And yet of Thee from year to year
The Church's solemn chant we hear,
As from Thy cradle to Thy throne
She swells her high heart-cheering tone.

Listen, ye pure white-robed souls,
Whom in her list she now enrolls,
And gird ye for your high emprize
By these her thrilling minstrelsies.

And wheresoe'er in earth's wide field,
Ye lift, for Him, the red-cross shield,
Be this your song, your joy and pride '
'Our Champion went before and died.'

TRINITY SUNDAY

If I have told you earthly things, and ye believe not, how shall ye
believe if I tell you of heavenly things? St. John iii. 12.

Creator, Saviour, strengthening Guide,
Now on Thy mercy's ocean wide
Far out of sight we seem to glide.

Help us, each hour, with steadier eye
To search the deepening mystery,
The wonders of Thy sea and sky.

The blessed Angels look and long
To praise Thee with a worthier song,
And yet our silence does Thee wrong. '

Along the Church's central space
The sacred weeks, with unfelt pace,
Hath borne us on from grace to grace.

As travellers on some woodland height,
When wintry suns are gleaming bright,
Lose in arch'd glades their tangled sight; -

By glimpses such as dreamers love
Through her grey veil the leafless grove
Shows where the distant shadows rove; -

Such trembling joy the soul o'er-awes
As nearer to Thy shrine she draws: '
And now before the choir we pause.

The door is clos'd - but soft and deep
Around the awful arches sweep,
Such airs as soothe a hermit's sleep.

From each carv'd nook and fretted bend
Cornice and gallery seem to send
Tones that with seraphs hymns might blend.

Three solemn parts together twine
In harmony's mysterious line;
Three solemn aisles approach the shrine:

Yet all are One - together all,
In thoughts that awe but not appal,
Teach the adoring heart to fall.

Within these walls each fluttering guest
Is gently lur'd to one safe nest '
Without, 'tis moaning and unrest.

The busy world a thousand ways
Is hurrying by, nor ever stays
To catch a note of Thy dear praise.

Why tarries not her chariot wheel,
That o'er her with no vain appeal
One gust of heavenly song might steal?

Alas! for her Thy opening flowers
Unheeded breathe to summer showers,
Unheard the music of Thy bowers.

What echoes from the sacred dome

The selfish spirit may o'ercome
That will not hear of love or home!

The heart that scorn'd a father's care,
How can it rise in filial prayer?
How an all-seeing Guardian bear?

Or how shall envious brethren own
A Brother on the eternal throne,
Their Father's joy, their hops alone?

How shall Thy Spirit's gracious wile
The sullen brow of gloom beguile,
That frowns on sweet Affection's smile?

Eternal One, Almighty Trine!
(Since Thou art ours, and we are Thine,)
By all Thy love did once resign,

By all the grace Thy heavens still hide,
We pray Thee, keep us at Thy side,
Creator, Saviour, strengthening Guide!

FIRST SUNDAY AFTER TRINITY

*So Joshua smote all the country, . . . and all their kings; he left
none remaining. Joshua x. 40.*

Where is the land with milk and honey flowing,
The promise of our God, our fancy's theme?
Here over shatter'd walls dank weeds are growing,
And blood and fire have run in mingled stream;
Like oaks and cedars all around
The giant corses strew the ground,
And haughty Jericho's cloud-piercing wall
Lies where it sank at Joshua's trumpet call.

These are not scenes for pastoral dance at even,
For moonlight rovings in the fragrant glades,
Soft slumbers in the open eye of Heaven,
And all the listless joy of summer shades.
We in the midst of ruins live,
Which every hour dread warning give,
Nor may our household vine or fig-tree hide
The broken arches of old Canaan's pride.

Where is the sweet repose of hearts repenting,
The deep calm sky, the sunshine of the soul,
Now Heaven and earth are to our bliss consenting,
And all the Godhead joins to make us whole.
The triple crown of mercy now
Is ready for the suppliant's brow,
By the Almighty Three for ever plann'd,

And from behind the cloud held out by Jesus' hand.

'Now, Christians, hold your own - the land before ye
Is open - win your way, and take your rest.'
So sounds our war-note; but our path of glory
By many a cloud is darken'd and unblest:
And daily as we downward glide,
Life's ebbing stream on either side
Shows at each turn some mouldering hope or joy,
The Man seems following still the funeral of the Boy.

Open our eyes, Thou Sun of life and gladness,
That we may see that glorious world of Thine!
It shines for us in vain, while drooping sadness
Enfolds us here like mist: come Power benign,
Touch our chill'd hearts with vernal smile,
Our wintry course do Thou beguile,
Nor by the wayside ruins let us mourn,
Who have th' eternal towers for our appointed bourne.

SECOND SUNDAY AFTER TRINITY

Marvel not, my brethren, if the world hate you. We know that
we have passed from death unto life, because we love the breth-
ren. 1 St. John iii. 13, 14.

The clouds that wrap the setting sun
When Autumn's softest gleams are ending,
Where all bright hues together run
In sweet confusion blending: '
Why, as we watch their floating wreath
Seem they the breath of life to breathe?
To Fancy's eye their motions prove
They mantle round the Sun for love.

When up some woodland dale we catch
The many-twinkling smile of ocean,
Or with pleas'd ear bewilder'd watch
His chime of restless motion;
Still as the surging waves retire
They seem to gasp with strong desire,
Such signs of love old Ocean gives,
We cannot choose but think he lives.

Wouldst thou the life of souls discern?
Nor human wisdom nor divine
Helps thee by aught beside to learn;
Love is life's only sign.
The spring of the regenerate heart,
The pulse, the glow of every part,

Is the true love of Christ our Lord,
As man embrac'd, as God ador'd.

But he, whose heart will bound to mark
The full bright burst of summer morn,
Loves too each little dewy spark,
By leaf or flow'ret worn:
Cheap forms, and common hues, 'tis true,
Through the bright shower-drop' meet his view;
The colouring may be of this earth;
The lustre comes of heavenly birth.

E'en so, who loves the Lord aright,
No soul of man can worthless find;
All will be precious in his sight,
Since Christ on all hath shin'd:
But chiefly Christian souls; for they,
Though worn and soil'd with sinful clay,
Are yet, to eyes that see them true,
All glistening with baptismal dew.

Then marvel not, if such as bask
In purest light of innocence,
Hope against mope, in love's dear task,
Spite of all dark offence.
If they who hate the trespass most,
Yet, when all other love is lost,
Love the poor sinner, marvel not;
Christ's mark outwears the rankest blot.

No distance breaks this tie of blood;
Brothers are brothers evermore;
Nor wrong, nor wrath of deadliest mood,
That magic may o'erpower;
Oft, ere the common source be known,
The kindred drops will claim their own,
And throbbing pulses silently

Move heart towards heart by sympathy.

So it is with true Christian hearts;
Their mutual share in Jesus' blood
An everlasting bond imparts
Of holiest brotherhood:
Oh! might we all our lineage prove,
Give and forgive, do good and love,
By soft endearments in kind strife
Lightening the load of daily life.

There is much need; for not as yet
Are we in shelter or repose,
The holy house is still beset
With leaguer of stern foes;
Wild thoughts within, bad men without,
All evil spirits round about,
Are banded in unblest device,
To spoil Love's earthly paradise.

Then draw we nearer day by day,
Each to his brethren, all to God;
Let the world take us as she may,
We must not change our road;
Not wondering, though in grief, to find
The martyr's foe still keep her mind;
But fix'd to hold Love's banner fast,
And by submission win at last.

THIRD SUNDAY AFTER TRINITY

There is joy in the presence of the angels of God over one sinner
that repenteth. St. Luke xv. 10.

O hateful spell of Sin! when friends are nigh,
To make stern Memory tell her tale unsought,
And raise accusing shades of hours gone by,
To come between us and all kindly thought!

Chill'd at her touch, the self-reproaching soul
Flies from the heart and home she dearest loves,
To where lone mountains tower, or billows roll,
Or to your endless depth, ye solemn groves.

In vain: the averted cheek in loneliest dell
Is conscious of a gaze it cannot bear,
The leaves that rustle near us seem to tell
Our heart's sad secret to the silent air.

Nor is the dream untrue; for all around
The heavens are watching with their thousand eyes,
We cannot pass our guardian angel's bound,
Resign'd or sullen, he will hear our sighs.

He in the mazes of the budding wood
Is near, and mourns to see our thankless glance
Dwell coldly, where the fresh green earth is strew'd

With the first flowers that lead the vernal dance.

In wasteful bounty shower'd, they smile unseen,
    Unseen by man - but what if purer sprights
    By moonlight o'er their dewy bosoms lean
      To adore the Father of all gentle lights?

If such there be, O grief and shame to think
    That sight of thee should overcloud their joy,
    A new-born soul, just waiting on the brink
    Of endless life, yet wrapt in earth's annoy!

O turn, and be thou turn'd! the selfish tear,
    In bitter thoughts of low-born care begun,
    Let it flow on, but flow refin'd and clear,
    The turbid waters brightening as they run.

Let it flow on, till all thine earthly heart
    In penitential drops have ebb'd away,
Then fearless turn where Heaven hath set thy part,
    Nor shudder at the Eye that saw thee stray.

O lost and found! all gentle souls below
    Their dearest welcome shall prepare, and prove
    Such joy o'er thee, as raptur'd seraphs know,
    Who learn their lesson at the Throne of Love.

FOURTH SUNDAY AFTER TRINITY

For the earnest expectation of the creature waiteth for the manifestation of the sons of God. For the creature was made subject to vanity, not willingly, but by the reason of Him who hath subjected the same in hope, because the creature itself also shall be delivered from the bondage of corruption into the glorious liberty of the children of God. For we know that the whole creation groaneth and travaileth in pain together until now.
Romans viii. 19-22.

It was not then a poet's dream,
An idle vaunt of song,
Such as beneath the moon's soft gleam
On vacant fancies throng;

Which bids us see in heaven and earth,
In all fair things around,
Strong yearnings for a blest new birth
With sinless glories crown'd;

Which bids us hear, at each sweet pause
From care and want and toil,
When dewy eve her curtain draws
Over the day's turmoil,

In the low chant of wakeful birds,
In the deep weltering flood,
In whispering leaves, these solemn words '

KEBLE

'God made us all for good.'

All true, all faultless, all in tune
 Creation's wondrous choir,
Open'd in mystic unison
 To last till time expire.

And still it lasts; by day and night,
 With one consenting voice,
All hymn Thy glory, Lord, aright,
 All worship and rejoice.

Man only mars the sweet accord
 O'erpowering with 'harsh din'
The music of Thy works and word,
 Ill matched with grief and sin.

Sin is with man at morning break,
 And through the livelong day
Deafens the ear that fain would wake
 To Nature's simple lay.

But when eve's silent footfall steals
 Along the eastern sky,
And one by one to earth reveals
 Those purer fires on high,

When one by one each human sound
 Dies on the awful ear,
Then Nature's voice no more is drown'd,
 She speaks, and we must hear.

Then pours she on the Christian heart
 That warning still and deep,
At which high spirits of old would start
 E'en from their Pagan sleep.

Just guessing, through their murky blind
Few, faint, and baffling sight,
Streaks of a brighter heaven behind,
A cloudless depth of light.

Such thoughts, the wreck of Paradise,
Through many a dreary age,
Upbore whate'er of good and wise
Yet liv'd in bard or sage:

They mark'd what agonizing throes
Shook the great mother's womb:
But Reason's spells might not disclose
The gracious birth to come:

Nor could th' enchantress Hope forecast
God's secret love and power;
The travail pangs of Earth must last
Till her appointed hour.

The hour that saw from opening heaven
Redeeming glory stream,
Beyond the summer hues of even,
Beyond the mid-day beam.

Thenceforth, to eyes of high desire,
The meanest thing below,
As with a seraph's robe of fire
Invested, burn and glow:

The rod of Heaven has touched them all,
The word from Heaven is spoken:
'Rise, shine, and sing, thou captive thrall;
Are not thy fetters broken?

'The God Who hallow'd thee and blest,
Pronouncing thee all good '

Hath He not all thy wrongs redrest,
And all thy bliss renew'd?

'Why mourn'st thou still as one bereft,
Now that th' eternal Son
His blessed home in Heaven hath left
To make thee all His own?'

Thou mourn'st because sin lingers still
In Christ's new heaven and earth;
Because our rebel works and will
Stain our immortal birth:

Because, as Love and Prayer grow cold,
The Saviour hides His face,
And worldlings blot the temple's gold
With uses vile and base.

Hence all thy groans and travail pains,
Hence, till thy God return,
In Wisdom's ear thy blithest strains,
Oh Nature, seem to mourn.

FIFTH SUNDAY AFTER TRINITY

And Simon answering said unto Him, Master, we have toiled all
the night, and have taken nothing; nevertheless at Thy word I
will let down the net. And when they had this done, they in-
closed a great multitude of fishes: and their net brake.
St. Luke v. 5, 6.

'The livelong night we've toil'd in vain,
But at Thy gracious word
I will let down the net again: '
Do Thou Thy will, O Lord!'

So spake the weary fisher, spent
With bootless darkling toil,
Yet on his Master's bidding bent
For love and not for spoil.

So day by day and week by week,
In sad and weary thought,
They muse, whom God hath set to seek
The souls His Christ hath bought.

For not upon a tranquil lake
Our pleasant task we ply,
Where all along our glistening wake
The softest moonbeams lie;

Where rippling wave and dashing oar
Our midnight chant attend,
Or whispering palm-leaves from the shore
With midnight silence blend.

Sweet thoughts of peace, ye may not last:
Too soon some ruder sound
Calls us from where ye soar so fast
Back to our earthly round.

For wildest storms our ocean sweep: '
No anchor but the Cross
Might hold: and oft the thankless deep
Turns all our toil to loss.

Full many a dreary anxious hour
We watch our nets alone
In drenching spray, and driving shower,
And hear the night-bird's moan:

At morn we look, and nought is there;
Sad dawn of cheerless day!
Who then from pining and despair
The sickening heart can stay?

There is a stay - and we are strong;
Our Master is at hand,
To cheer our solitary song,
And guide us to the strand.

In His own time; but yet a while
Our bark at sea must ride;
Cast after cast, by force or guile
All waters must be tried:

By blameless guile or gentle force,
As when He deign'd to teach

(The lode-star of our Christian course)
Upon this sacred beach.

Should e'er thy wonder-working grace
Triumph by our weak arm,
Let not our sinful fancy trace
Aught human in the charm:

To our own nets [72] ne'er bow we down,
Lest on the eternal shore
The angels, while oar draught they own, [73]
Reject us evermore:

Or, if for our unworthiness
Toil, prayer, and watching fail,
In disappointment Thou canst bless,
So love at heart prevail.

[72] They sacrifice unto their net, and burn incense unto their drag.Habakkuk i. 16.
[73] St. Matthew xiii. 49

SIXTH SUNDAY AFTER TRINITY

David said unto Nathan, I have sinned against the Lord. And Nathan said unto David, The Lord also hath put away thy sin; thou shalt not die. 2 Samuel xii. 13.

When bitter thoughts, of conscience born,
With sinners wake at morn,
When from our restless couch we start,
With fever'd lips and wither'd heart,
Where is the spell to charm those mists away,
And make new morning in that darksome day?
One draught of spring's delicious air,
One steadfast thought, that GOD is there.

These are Thy wonders, hourly wrought, [74]
Thou Lord of time and thought,
Lifting and lowering souls at will,
Crowding a world of good or ill
Into a moment's vision; e'en as light
Mounts o'er a cloudy ridge, and all is bright,
From west to east one thrilling ray
Turning a wintry world to May.

Would'st thou the pangs of guilt assuage?
Lo! here an open page,
Where heavenly mercy shines as free
Written in balm, sad heart, for thee.
Never so fast, in silent April shower,

Flush'd into green the dry and leafless bower, [75]
   As Israel's crowned mourner felt
   The dull hard stone within him melt.

   The absolver saw the mighty grief,
     And hasten'd with relief; -
'The Lord forgives; thou shalt not die:'
'Twas gently spoke, yet heard on high,
And all the band of angels, us'd to sing
In heaven, accordant to his raptur'd string,
   Who many a month had turn'd away
   With veiled eyes, nor own'd his lay,

Now spread their wings, and throng around
     To the glad mournful sound,
   And welcome, with bright open face,
   The broken heart to love's embrace.
The rock is smitten, and to future years
Springs ever fresh the tide of holy tears [76]
   And holy music, whispering peace
   Till time and sin together cease.

   There drink: and when ye are at rest,
     With that free Spirit blest, [77]
   Who to the contrite can dispense,
   The princely heart of innocence,
If ever, floating from faint earthly lyre,
Was wafted to your soul one high desire,
   By all the trembling hope ye feel,
   Think on the minstrel as ye kneel:

   Think on the shame, that dreadful hour
     When tears shall have no power,
   Should his own lay th' accuser prove,
   Cold while he kindled others' love:
And let your prayer for charity arise,
That his own heart may hear his melodies,

And a true voice to him may cry,
'Thy GOD forgives - thou shalt not die.'

[74] See Herber's Poems, p. 160.

[75] And all this leafless and uncolour'd sense Shall flash into variety again. Cowper.

[76] The fifty-first Psalm.

[77] Psalm li. 12. 'Uphold me with thy free Spirit.' The original word seems to mean 'ingenuous, princely, noble.' Read Bishop Horne's paraphrase on the verse.

SEVENTH SUNDAY AFTER TRINITY

From whence can a man satisfy these men with bread here in the
wilderness? St. Mark viii. 4.

Go not away, thou weary soul:
Heaven has in store a precious dole
Here on Bethsaida's cold and darksome height,
Where over rocks and sands arise
Proud Sirion in the northern skies,
And Tabor's lonely peak, 'twixt thee and noonday light.

And far below, Gennesaret's main
Spreads many a mile of liquid plain,
(Though all seem gather'd in one eager bound,)
Then narrowing cleaves you palmy lea,
Towards that deep sulphureous sea,
Where five proud cities lie, by one dire sentence drown'd.

Landscape of fear! yet, weary heart,
Thou need'st not in thy gloom depart,
Nor fainting turn to seek thy distant home:
Sweetly thy sickening throbs are ey'd
By the kind Saviour at thy side;
For healing and for balm e'en now thine hour is come.

No fiery wing is seen to glide,
No cates ambrosial are supplied,
But one poor fisher's rude and scanty store

Is all He asks (and more than needs)
Who men and angels daily feeds,
And stills the wailing sea-bird on the hungry shore.

The feast is o'er, the guests are gone,
And over all that upland lone
The breeze of eve sweeps wildly as of old '
But far unlike the former dreams,
The heart's sweet moonlight softly gleams
Upon life's varied view, so joyless erst and cold.

As mountain travellers in the night,
When heaven by fits is dark and bright,
Pause listening on the silent heath, and hear
Nor trampling hoof nor tinkling bell,
Then bolder scale the rugged fell,
Conscious the more of One, ne'er seen, yet ever near:

So when the tones of rapture gay
On the lorn ear, die quite away,
The lonely world seems lifted nearer heaven;
Seen daily, yet unmark'd before,
Earth's common paths are strewn all o'er
With flowers of pensive hope, the wreath of man forgiven.

The low sweet tones of Nature's lyre
No more on listless ears expire,
Nor vainly smiles along the shady way
The primrose in her vernal nest,
Nor unlamented sink to rest
Sweet roses one by one, nor autumn leaves decay.

There's not a star the heaven can show,
There's not a cottage-hearth below,
But feeds with solace kind the willing soul '
Men love us, or they need our love;
Freely they own, or heedless prove

The curse of lawless hearts, the joy of self-control.

Then rouse thee from desponding sleep,
Nor by the wayside lingering weep,
Nor fear to seek Him farther in the wild,
Whose love can turn earth's worst and least
Into a conqueror's royal feast:
Thou wilt not be untrue, thou shalt not be beguil'd.

EIGHTH SUNDAY AFTER TRINITY

It is the man of God, who was disobedient unto the word of the
Lord. 1 Kings xiii. 26.

Prophet of God, arise and take
With thee the words of wrath divine,
The scourge of Heaven, to shake
O'er yon apostate shrine.

Where Angels down the lucid stair
Came hovering to our sainted sires
Now, in the twilight, glare
The heathen's wizard fires.

Go, with thy voice the altar rend,
Scatter the ashes, be the arm,
That idols would befriend,
Shrunk at thy withering charm.

Then turn thee, for thy time is short,
But trace not o'er the former way,
Lest idol pleasures court
Thy heedless soul astray.

Thou know'st how hard to hurry by,
Where on the lonely woodland road
Beneath the moonlight sky

The festal warblings flow'd;

Where maidens to the Queen of Heaven
Wove the gay dance round oak or palm,
    Or breath'd their vows at even
    In hymns as soft as balm.

Or thee, perchance, a darker spell
Enthralls: the smooth stones of the flood, [78]
    By mountain grot or fell,
    Pollute with infant's blood;

The giant altar on the rock,
The cavern whence the timbrel's call
    Affrights the wandering flock: '
    Thou long'st to search them all.

Trust not the dangerous path again '
O forward step and lingering will!
    O lov'd and warn'd in vain!
    And wilt thou perish still?

Thy message given, thine home in sight,
    To the forbidden feast return?
    Yield to the false delight
    Thy better soul could spurn?

Alas, my brother! round thy tomb
In sorrow kneeling, and in fear,
    We read the Pastor's doom
    Who speaks and will not hear.

The grey-hair'd saint may fail at last,
The surest guide a wanderer prove;
    Death only binds us fast
    To the bright shore of love.

[78] Among the smooth stones of the stream is thy portion; they, they are thy lot. Isaiah lvii. 6.

NINTH SUNDAY AFTER TRINITY

And after the earthquake a fire; but the Lord was not in the fire:
and after the fire a still small voice. 1 Kings xix. 12.

In troublous days of anguish and rebuke,
While sadly round them Israel's children look,
And their eyes fail for waiting on their Lord:
While underneath each awful arch of green,
On every mountain-top, God's chosen scene,
Of pure heart-worship, Baal is ador'd:

'Tis well, true hearts should for a time retire
To holy ground, in quiet to aspire
Towards promis'd regions of serener grace;
On Horeb, with Elijah, let us lie,
Where all around on mountain, sand, and sky,
God's chariot wheels have left distinctest trace;

There, if in jealousy and strong disdain
We to the sinner's God of sin complain,
Untimely seeking here the peace of Heaven '
'It is enough. O Lord! now let me die
E'en as my fathers did: for what am I
That I should stand where they have vainly striven?' '

Perhaps our God may of our conscience ask,
'What doest thou here frail wanderer from thy task?
Where hast thou left those few sheep in the wild?' [79]
Then should we plead our heart's consuming pain,

At sight of ruin'd altars, prophets slain,
And God's own ark with blood of souls defil'd;

He on the rock may bid us stand, and see
The outskirts of His march of mystery,
His endless warfare with man's wilful heart;
First, His great Power He to the sinner shows
Lo! at His angry blast the rocks unclose,
And to their base the trembling mountains part

Yet the Lord is not here: 'tis not by Power
He will be known - but darker tempests lower;
Still, sullen heavings vex the labouring ground:
Perhaps His Presence thro' all depth and height,
Best of all gems that deck His crown of light,
The haughty eye may dazzle and confound.

God is not in the earthquake; but behold
From Sinai's caves are bursting, as of old,
The flames of His consuming jealous ire.
Woe to the sinner should stern Justice prove
His chosen attribute; - but He in love
Hastes to proclaim, 'God is not in the fire.'

The storm is o'er - and hark! a still small voice
Steals on the ear, to say, Jehovah's choice
Is ever with the soft, meek, tender soul;
By soft, meek, tender ways He loves to draw
The sinner, startled by His ways of awe:
Here is our Lord, and not where thunders roll.

Back, then, complainer; loath thy life no more,
Nor deem thyself upon a desert shore,
Because the rocks the nearer prospect close.
Yet in fallen Israel are there hearts and eyes
That day by day in prayer like thine arise;
Thou know'st them not, but their Creator knows.

Go, to the world return, nor fear to cast
Thy bread upon the waters, sure at last [80]
In joy to find it after many days.
The work be thine, the fruit thy children's part:
Choose to believe, not see: sight tempts the heart
From sober walking in true Gospel ways.

[79] 1 Samuel xvii. 28.
[80] Ecclesiastes xi. 1.

TENTH SUNDAY AFTER TRINITY

And when He was come near, He beheld the city, and wept over
it. St. Luke xix. 41.

Why doth my Saviour weep
At sight of Sion's bowers?
Shows it not fair from yonder steep,
Her gorgeous crown of towers?
Mark well His holy pains:
'Tis not in pride or scorn,
That Israel's King with sorrow stains
His own triumphal morn.

It is not that His soul
Is wandering sadly on,
In thought how soon at death's dark goal
Their course will all be run,
Who now are shouting round
Hosanna to their chief;
No thought like this in Him is found,
This were a Conquerer's grief. [81]

Or doth He feel the Cross
Already in His heart,
The pain, the shame, the scorn, the loss?
Feel e'en His God depart?
No: though He knew full well
The grief that then shall be '

The grief that angels cannot tell '
Our God in agony.

It is not thus He mourns;
Such might be martyr's tears,
When his last lingering look he turns
On human hopes and fears;
But hero ne'er or saint
The secret load might know,
With which His spirit waxeth faint;
His is a Saviour's woe.

'If thou had'st known, e'en thou,
At least in this thy day,
The message of thy peace! but now
'Tis pass'd for aye away:
Now foes shall trench thee round,
And lay thee even with earth,
And dash thy children to the ground,
Thy glory and thy mirth.'

And doth the Saviour weep
Over His people's sin,
Because we will not let Him keep
The souls He died to win?
Ye hearts, that love the Lord,
If at this, sight ye burn,
See that in thought, in deed, in word,
Ye hate what made Him mourn.

[81] Compare Herod. vii. 46.

ELEVENTH SUNDAY AFTER TRINITY

Is it a time to receive money, and to receive garments, and oliveyards, and vineyards, and sheep, and oxen, and menservants, and maidservants? 2 Kings v. 26.

Is this a time to plant and build,
Add house to house, and field to field,
When round our walls the battle lowers,
When mines are hid beneath our towers,
And watchful foes are stealing round
To search and spoil the holy ground?

Is this a time for moonlight dreams
Of love and home by mazy streams,
For Fancy with her shadowy toys,
Aerial hopes and pensive joys,
While souls are wandering far and wide,
And curses swarm on every side?

No - rather steel thy melting heart
To act the martyr's sternest part,
To watch, with firm unshrinking eye,
Thy darling visions as thy die,
Till all bright hopes, and hues of day,
Have faded into twilight gray.

Yes - let them pass without a sigh,

And if the world seem dull and dry,
If long and sad thy lonely hours,
And winds have rent thy sheltering bowers,
Bethink thee what thou art and where,
A sinner in a life of care.

The fire of God is soon to fall
(Thou know'st it) on this earthly ball;
Full many a soul, the price of blood,
Mark'd by th' Almighty's hand for good,
To utter death that hour shall sweep '
And will the saints in Heaven dare weep?

Then in His wrath shall GOD uproot
The trees He set, for lack of fruit,
And drown in rude tempestuous blaze
The towers His hand had deign'd to raise;
In silence, ere that storm begin,
Count o'er His mercies and thy sin.

Pray only that thine aching heart,
From visions vain content to part,
Strong for Love's sake its woe to hide
May cheerful wait the Cross beside,
Too happy if, that dreadful day,
Thy life be given thee for a prey. [82]

Snatch'd sudden from th' avenging rod,
Safe in the bosom of thy GOD,
How wilt thou then look back, and smile
On thoughts that bitterest seem'd erewhile,
And bless the pangs that made thee see
This was no world of rest for thee!

[82] The Lord saith thus: Behold, that which I have built will I
break down, and that which I have planted I will pluck up, even
this whole land. And seekest thou great things for thyself? seek

them not: for, behold, I will bring evil upon all flesh, saith the Lord: but thy life will I give unto thee for a prey in all places whither thou goest. Jeremiah xlv. 4, 5.

TWELFTH SUNDAY AFTER TRINITY

And looking up to heaven, He sighed, and saith unto him, Eph-
phatha, that is, Be opened. St. Mark vii. 34.

The Son of God in doing good
Was fain to look to Heaven and sigh:
And shall the heirs of sinful blood
Seek joy unmix'd in charity?
God will not let Love's work impart
Full solace, lest it steal the heart;
Be thou content in tears to sow,
Blessing, like Jesus, in thy woe:

He look'd to Heaven, and sadly sigh'd '
What saw my gracious Saviour there,
'With fear and anguish to divide
The joy of Heaven-accepted prayer?
So o'er the bed where Lazarus slept
He to His Father groaned and wept:
What saw He mournful in that grave,
Knowing Himself so strong to save?'

O'erwhelming thoughts of pain and grief
Over His sinking spirit sweep; -
What boots it gathering one lost leaf
Out of yon sere and wither'd heap,
Where souls and bodies, hopes and joys,
All that earth owns or sin destroys,

Under the spurning hoof are cast,
Or tossing in th' autumnal blast?

The deaf may hear the Saviour's voice,
The fetter'd tongue its chain may break;
But the deaf heart, the dumb by choice,
The laggard soul, that will not wake,
The guilt that scorns to be forgiven; -
These baffle e'en the spells of Heaven;
In thought of these, His brows benign
Not e'en in healing cloudless shine.

No eye but His might ever bear
To gaze all down that drear abyss,
Because none ever saw so clear
The shore beyond of endless bliss:
The giddy waves so restless hurl'd,
The vex'd pulse of this feverish world,
He views and counts with steady sight,
Used to behold the Infinite.

But that in such communion high
He hath a fount of strength within,
Sure His meek heart would break and die,
O'erburthen'd by His brethren's sin;
Weak eyes on darkness dare not gaze,
It dazzles like the noonday blaze;
But He who sees God's face may brook
On the true face of Sin to look.

What then shall wretched sinners do,
When in their last, their hopeless day,
Sin, as it is, shall meet their view,
God turn His face for aye away?
Lord, by Thy sad and earnest eye,
When Thou didst look to Heaven and sigh:
Thy voice, that with a word could chase

The dumb, deaf spirit from his place;

As Thou hast touch'd our ears, and taught
Our tongues to speak Thy praises plain,
Quell Thou each thankless godless thought
That would make fast our bonds again.
From worldly strife, from mirth unblest,
Drowning Thy music in the breast,
From foul reproach, from thrilling fears,
Preserve, good Lord, Thy servants' ears.

From idle words, that restless throng
And haunt our hearts when we would pray,
From Pride's false chime, and jarring wrong,
Seal Thou my lips, and guard the way:
For Thou hast sworn, that every ear,
Willing or loth, Thy trump shall hear,
And every tongue unchained be
To own no hope, no God, but Thee.

THIRTEENTH SUNDAY AFTER TRINITY

And He turned Him onto His disciples, and said privately,
Blessed are the eyes which see the things that ye see: for I tell
you, that many prophets and kings have desired to see those
things which ye see, and have not seen them: and to hear those
things which ye hear, and have not heard them.
St.Luke x. 23, 24.

On Sinai's top, in prayer and trance,
Full forty nights and forty days
The Prophet watch'd for one dear glance
Of thee and of Thy ways:

Fasting he watch'd and all alone,
Wrapt in a still, dark, solid cloud,
The curtain of the Holy One
Drawn round him like a shroud:

So, separate from the world, his breast
Might duly take and strongly keep
The print of Heaven, to be express'd
Ere long on Sion's steep. [83]

There one by one his spirit saw
Of things divine the shadows bright,
The pageant of God's perfect law;
Yet felt not full delight.

Through gold and gems, a dazzling maze,
From veil to veil the vision led,
And ended, where unearthly rays
From o'er the ark were shed.

Yet not that gorgeous place, nor aught
Of human or angelic frame,
Could half appease his craving thought;
The void was still the same.

'Show me Thy glory, gracious Lord!
'Tis Thee,' he cries, 'not Thine, I seek.' [84]
Na, start not at so bold a word
From man, frail worm and weak:

The spark of his first deathless fire
Yet buoys him up, and high above
The holiest creature, dares aspire
To the Creator's love.

The eye in smiles may wander round,
Caught by earth's shadows as they fleet;
But for the soul no help is found,
Save Him who made it, meet.

Spite of yourselves, ye witness this, [85]
Who blindly self or sense adore;
Else wherefore leaving your own bliss
Still restless ask ye more?

This witness bore the saints of old
When highest rapt and favour'd most,
Still seeking precious things untold,
Not in fruition lost.

Canaan was theirs; and in it all
The proudest hope of kings dare claim:

Sion was theirs; and at their call
Fire from Jehovah came.

Yet monarchs walk'd as pilgrims still
In their own land, earth's pride and grace:
And seers would mourn on Sion's hill
Their Lord's averted face.

Vainly they tried the deeps to sound
E'en of their own prophetic thought,
When of Christ crucified and crown'd
His Spirit in them taught:

But He their aching gaze repress'd,
Which sought behind the veil to see,
For not without us fully bles'd [86]
Or perfect might they be.

The rays of the Almighty's face
No sinner's eye might then receive;
Only the meekest man found grace [87]
To see His skirts and live.

But we as in a glass espy
The glory of His countenance,
Not in a whirlwind hurrying by
The too presumptuous glance,

But with mild radiance every hour,
From our dear Saviour's face benign
Bent on us with transforming power,
Till we, too, faintly shine.

Sprinkled with His atoning blood
Safely before our God we stand,
As on the rock the Prophet stood,
Beneath His shadowing hand. '

Bless'd eyes, which see the things we see!
And yet this tree of life hath prov'd
To many a soul a poison tree,
Beheld, and not belov'd.

So like an angel's is our bliss
(Oh! thought to comfort and appal)
It needs must bring, if us'd amiss,
An angel's hopeless fall.

[83] See that thou make all things according to the pattern shewed to thee in the mount. Hebrews viii. 5.
[84] Exodus xxxiii. 18.
[85] PensÃ©es de Pascal, part 1, art. viii.
[86] That they without us should not be made perfect. Hebrews xi. 40.
[87] Exodus xxxiii. 20-23.

FOURTEENTH SUNDAY AFTER TRINITY

And Jesus answering said, Were there not ten cleansed? but
where are the nine? There are not found that returned to give
glory to God, save this stranger.
St. Luke xvii. 17, 18.

Ten cleans'd, and only one remain!
Who would have thought our nature's stain
Was dyed so foul, so deep in grain?
E'en He who reads the heart '
Knows what He gave and what we lost,
Sin's forfeit, and redemption's cost, '
By a short pang of wonder cross'd
Seems at the sight to start:

Yet 'twas not wonder, but His love
Our wavering spirits would reprove,
That heavenward seem so free to move
When earth can yield no more
Then from afar on God we cry,
But should the mist of woe roll by,
Not showers across an April sky
Drift, when the storm is o'er,

Faster than those false drops and few
Fleet from the heart, a worthless dew.

What sadder scene can angels view
Than self-deceiving tears,
Pour'd idly over some dark page
Of earlier life, though pride or rage,
The record of to-day engage,
A woe for future years?

Spirits, that round the sick man's bed
Watch'd, noting down each prayer he made,
Were your unerring roll displayed,
His pride of health to' abase;
Or, when, soft showers in season fall
Answering a famish'd nation's call,
Should unseen fingers on the wall
Our vows forgotten trace:

How should we gaze in trance of fear!
Yet shines the light as thrilling clear
From Heaven upon that scroll severe,
'Ten cleans'd and one remain!'
Nor surer would the blessing prove
Of humbled hearts, that own Thy love,
Should choral welcome from above
Visit our senses plain:

Than by Thy placid voice and brow,
With healing first, with comfort now,
Turn'd upon him, who hastes to bow
Before Thee, heart and knee;
'Oh! thou, who only wouldst be blest,
On thee alone My blessing rest!
Rise, go thy way in peace, possess'd
For evermore of Me.'

FIFTEENTH SUNDAY AFTER TRINITY

Consider the lilies of the field, how they grow.
St. Matthew vi. 28.

Sweet nurslings of the vernal skies,
Bath'd in soft airs, and fed with dew,
What more than magic in you lies,
To fill the heart's fond view?
In childhood's sports, companions gay,
In sorrow, on Life's downward way,
How soothing! in our last decay
Memorials prompt and true.

Relics ye are of Eden's bowers,
As pure, as fragrant, and as fair,
As when ye crown'd the sunshine hours
Of happy wanderers there.
Fall'n all beside - the world of life,
How is it stain'd with fear and strife!
In Reason's world what storms are rife,
What passions range and glare!

But cheerful and unchang'd the while
Your first and perfect form ye show,
The same that won Eve's matron smile
In the world's opening glow.
The stars of heaven a course are taught
Too high above our human thought:
Ye may be found if ye are sought,

And as we gaze, we know.

Ye dwell beside our paths and homes,
Our paths of sin, our homes of sorrow,
And guilty man where'er he roams,
Your innocent mirth may borrow.
The birds of air before us fleet,
They cannot brook our shame to meet '
But we may taste your solace sweet
And come again to-morrow.

Ye fearless in your nests abide '
Nor may we scorn, too proudly wise,
Your silent lessons, undescried
By all but lowly eyes:
For ye could draw th' admiring gaze
Of Him who worlds and hearts surveys:
Your order wild, your fragrant maze,
He taught us how to prize.

Ye felt your Maker's smile that hour,
As when He paus'd and own'd you good;
His blessing on earth's primal bower,
Ye felt it all renew'd.
What care ye now, if winter's storm
Sweep ruthless o'er each silken form?
Christ's blessing at your heart is warm,
Ye fear no vexing mood.

Alas! of thousand bosoms kind,
That daily court you and caress,
How few the happy secret find
Of your calm loveliness!
'Live for to-day! to-morrow's light
To-morrow's cares shall bring to sight,
Go sleep like closing flowers at night,
And Heaven thy morn will bless.'

SIXTEENTH SUNDAY AFTER TRINITY

I desire that ye faint not at my tribulations for you, which is your glory. Ephesians iii. 13.

Wish not, dear friends, my pain away '
Wish me a wise and thankful heart,
With GOD, in all my griefs, to stay,
Nor from His lov'd correction start.

The dearest offering He can crave
His portion in our souls to prove,
What is it to the gift He gave,
The only Son of His dear love?

But we, like vex'd unquiet sprights,
Will still be hovering o'er the tomb,
Where buried lie our vain delights,
Nor sweetly take a sinner's doom.

In Life's long sickness evermore
Our thoughts are tossing to and fro:
We change our posture o'er and o'er,
But cannot rest, nor cheat our woe.

Were it not better to lie still,
Let Him strike home and bless the rod,
Never so safe as when our will
Yields undiscern'd by all but God?

Thy precious things, whate'er they be,
That haunt and vex thee, heart and brain,
Look to the Cross and thou shalt see
How thou mayst turn them all to gain.

Lovest thou praise? the Cross is shame:
Or ease? the Cross is bitter grief:
More pangs than tongue or heart can frame
Were suffer'd there without relief.

We of that Altar would partake,
But cannot quit the cost - no throne
Is ours, to leave for Thy dear sake '
We cannot do as Thou hast done.

We cannot part with Heaven for Thee '
Yet guide us in Thy track of love:
Let us gaze on where light should be,
Though not a beam the clouds remove.

So wanderers ever fond and true
Look homeward through the evening sky,
Without a streak of heaven's soft blue
To aid Affection's dreaming eye.

The wanderer seeks his native bower,
And we will look and long for Thee,
And thank Thee for each trying hour,
Wishing, not struggling, to be free.

SEVENTEENTH SUNDAY AFTER TRINITY

Every man of the house of Israel that setteth up his idols in his heart, and putteth the stumbling-block of his iniquity before his face, and cometh to the prophet; I the Lord will answer him that cometh according to the multitude of his idols. Ezekiel xiv. 4.

> Stately thy walls, and holy are the prayers
> Which day and night before thine altars rise:
> Not statelier, towering o'er her marble stairs,
> Flash'd Sion's gilded dome to summer skies,
> Not holier, while around him angels bow'd,
> From Aaron's censer steam'd the spicy cloud,
>
> Before the mercy-seat. O Mother dear,
> Wilt thou forgive thy son one boding sigh?
> Forgive, if round thy towers he walk in fear,
> And tell thy jewels o'er with jealous eye?
> Mindful of that sad vision, which in thought [88]
> From Chebar's plains the captive prophet brought.
>
> To see lost Sion's shame. 'Twas morning prime,
> And like a Queen new seated on her throne,
> God'S crowned mountain, as in happier time,
> Seem'd to rejoice in sunshine all her own:
> So bright, while all in shade around her lay,
> Her northern pinnacles had caught th' emerging ray.

The dazzling lines of her majestic roof
Cross'd with as free a span the vault of heaven,
As when twelve tribes knelt silently aloof
Ere God His answer to their king had given, [89]
Ere yet upon the new-built altar fell
The glory of the Lord, the Lord of Israel.

All seems the same: but enter in and see
What idol shapes are on the wall portray'd: [90]
And watch their shameless and unholy glee,
Who worship there in Aaron's robes array'd:
Hear Judah's maids the dirge to Thammuz pour, [91]
And mark her chiefs yon orient sun adore. [92]

Yet turn thee, son of man - for worse than these
Thou must behold: thy loathing were but lost
On dead men's crimes, and Jews' idolatries '
Come, learn to tell aright thine own sins' cost, '
And sure their sin as far from equals thine,
As earthly hopes abus'd are less than hopes divine.

What if within His world, His Church, our Lord
Have enter'd thee, as in some temple gate,
Where, looking round, each glance might thee afford
Some glorious earnest of thine high estate,
And thou, false heart and frail, hast turn'd from all
To worship pleasure's shadow on the wall?

If, when the LORD of Glory was in sight,
Thou turn thy back upon that fountain clear,
To bow before the 'little drop of light,.'
Which dim-eyed men call praise and glory here;
What dost thou, but adore the sun, and scorn
Him at whose only word both sun and stars were born?

If, while around thee gales from Eden breathe,

Thou hide thine eyes, to make thy peevish moan
Over some broken reed of earth beneath,
Some darling of blind fancy dead and gone,
As wisely might'st thou in Jehovah'S fane
Offer thy love and tears to Thammuz slain.

Turn thee from these, or dare not to inquire
Of Him whose name is Jealous, lest in wrath
He hear and answer thine unblest desire:
Far better we should cross His lightning's path
Than be according to our idols beard,
And God should take us at our own vain word.

Thou who hast deign'd the Christian's heart to call
Thy Church and Shrine; whene'er our rebel will
Would in that chosen home of Thine instal
Belial or Mammon, grant us not the ill
We blindly ask; in very love refuse
Whate'er Thou know'st our weakness would abuse.

Or rather help us, Lord, to choose the good,
To pray for nought, to seek to none, but Thee,
Nor by 'our daily bread' mean common food,
Nor say, 'From this world's evil set us free;'
Teach us to love, with Christ, our sole true bliss,
Else, though in Christ'S own words, we surely pray amiss.

[88] Ezekiel viii. 3.
[89] 1 Kings viii. 5.
[90] Ezekiel viii. 10.
[91] Ezekiel viii. 14.
[92] Ezekiel viii. 16.

EIGHTEENTH SUNDAY AFTER TRINITY

I will bring you into the wilderness of the people, and there will
I plead with you face to face. Like as pleaded with your fathers
in the wilderness of the land of Egypt, so will I plead with you,
saith the Lord God. Ezekiel xx. 35, 36.

It is so - ope thine eyes, and see '
What viewest thou all around?
A desert, where iniquity
And knowledge both abound.

In the waste howling wilderness
The Church is wandering still, [93]
Because we would not onward press
When close to Sion's hill.

Back to the world we faithless turn'd,
And far along the wild,
With labour lost and sorrow earn'd,
Our steps have been beguil'd.

Yet full before us, all the while,
The shadowing pillar stays,
The living waters brightly smile,
The eternal turrets blaze,

Yet Heaven is raining angels' bread
To be our daily food,

And fresh, as when it first was shed,
Springs forth the Saviour's blood.

From every region, race, and speech,
Believing myriads throng,
Till, far as sin and sorrow reach,
Thy grace is spread along;

Till sweetest nature, brightest art,
Their votive incense bring,
And every voice and every heart
Own Thee their God and King.

All own; but few, alas! will love;
Too like the recreant band
That with Thy patient spirit strove
Upon the Red-sea strand.

O Father of long-suffering grace,
Thou who hast sworn to stay
Pleading with sinners face to face
Through all their devious way:

How shall we speak to Thee, O Lord,
Or how in silence lie?
Look on us, and we are abhorr'd,
Turn from us, and we die.

Thy guardian fire, Thy guiding cloud,
Still let them gild our wall,
Nor be our foes and Thine allow'd
To see us faint and fall.

Too oft, within this camp of Thine,
Rebellions murmurs rise;
Sin cannot bear to see Thee shine
So awful to her eyes.

Fain would our lawless hearts escape,
And with the heathen be,
To worship every monstrous shape
In fancied darkness free.

Vain thought, that shall not be at all! [94]
Refuse we or obey,
Our ears have heard the Almighty's call,
We cannot be as they.

We cannot hope the heathen's doom
To whom God's Son is given,
Whose eyes have seen beyond the tomb,
Who have the key of Heaven.

Weak tremblers on the edge of woe,
Yet shrinking from true bliss,
Our rest must be 'no rest below,.'
And let our prayer be this:

'Lord, wave again Thy chastening rod,
Till every idol throne
Crumble to dust, and Thou, O God,
Reign in our hearts alone.

'Bring all our wandering fancies home,
For Thou hast every spell,
And 'mid the heathen where they roam,
Thou know'st, Lord, too well.

'Thou know'st our service sad and hard,
Thou know'st us fond and frail;
Win us to be belov'd and spar'd
When all the world shall fail.

'So when at last our weary days

Are well-nigh wasted here,
And we can trace Thy wondrous ways
In distance calm and clear,

'When in Thy love and Israel's sin
We read our story true,
We may not, all too late, begin
To wish our hopes were new.

'Long lov'd, long tried, long spar'd as they,
Unlike in this alone,
That, by Thy grace, our hearts shall stay
For evermore Thine own.'

[93] Revelations xii. 14.
[94] That which cometh into your mind shall not be at all, that ye say, We will be as the heathen, as the families of the countries, to serve wood and stone. Ezekiel xx. 32.

NINETEENTH SUNDAY AFTER TRINITY

Then Nebuchadnezzar the king was astonished, and rose up in
haste, and spake, and said unto his counsellors, Did not we cast
three men bound into the midst of the fire? They answered and
said un to the king, True, O king. He answered and said, Lo, I
see four men loose, walking in the midst of the fire, and they
have no hurt; and the form of the fourth is like the Son of God.
Daniel iii. 24, 25.

When Persecution's torrent blaze
Wraps the unshrinking Martyr's head;
When fade all earthly flowers and bays,
When summer friends are gone and fled,
Is he alone in that dark hour
Who owns the Lord of love and power?

Or waves there not around his brow
A wand no human arm may wield,
Fraught with a spell no angels know,
His steps to guide, his soul to shield?
Thou, Saviour, art his Charmed Bower,
His Magic Ring, his Rock, his Tower.

And when the wicked ones behold
Thy favourites walking in Thy light,
Just as, in fancy triumph bold,
They deem'd them lost in deadly night,

Amaz'd they cry, 'What spell is this,
Which turns their sufferings all to bliss?

'How are they free whom we had bound?
Upright, whom in the gulf we cast?
What wondrous helper have they found
To screen them from the scorching blast?
Three were they - who hath made them four?
And sure a form divine he wore,

'E'en like the Son of God.' So cried
The Tyrant, when in one fierce flame
The Martyrs liv'd, the murderers died:
Yet knew he not what angel came
To make the rushing fire-flood seem
Like summer breeze by woodland stream. [95]

He knew not, but there are who know:
The Matron, who alone hath stood,
When not a prop seem'd left below,
The first lorn hour of widowhood,
Yet cheer'd and cheering all, the while,
With sad but unaffected smile; -

The Father, who his vigil keeps
By the sad couch whence hope hath flown,
Watching the eye where reason sleeps,
Yet in his heart can mercy own,
Still sweetly yielding to the rod,
Still loving man, still thanking God; -

The Christian Pastor, bow'd to earth
With thankless toil, and vile esteem'd,
Still travailing in second birth
Of souls that will not be redeem'd:
Yet stedfast set to do his part,
And fearing most his own vain heart; -

These know: on these look long and well,
Cleansing thy sight by prayer and faith,
And thou shalt know what secret spell
Preserves them in their living death:
Through sevenfold flames thine eye shall see
The Saviour walking with His faithful Three.

[95] As it had been a moist whistling wind. Song of the Three
Children, vers. 27.

TWENTIETH SUNDAY AFTER TRINITY

Hear ye, O mountains, the Lord's controversy, and ye strong
foundations of the earth. Micah vi. 2.

Where is Thy favour'd haunt, eternal Voice,
The region of Thy choice,
Where, undisturb'd by sin and earth, the soul
Owns Thy entire control? '
'Tis on the mountain's summit dark and high,
When storms are hurrying by:
'Tis 'mid the strong foundations of the earth,
Where torrents have their birth.

No sounds of worldly toil ascending there,
Mar the full burst of prayer;
Lone Nature feels that she may freely breathe,
And round us and beneath
Are heard her sacred tones: the fitful sweep
Of winds across the steep
Through wither'd bents - romantic note and clear,
Meet for a hermit's ear, '

The wheeling kite's wild solitary cry,
And, scarcely heard so high,
The dashing waters when the air is still
From many a torrent rill
That winds unseen beneath the shaggy fell,
Track'd by the blue mist well:

Such sounds as make deep silence in the heart
For Thought to do her part.

'Tis then we hear the voice of GOD within,
Pleading with care and sin:
'Child of My love! how have I wearied thee?
Why wilt thou err from Me?
Have I not brought thee from the house of slaves,
Parted the drowning waves,
And set My saints before thee in the way,
Lest thou shouldst faint or stray?

'What! was the promise made to thee alone?
Art thou th' excepted one?
An heir of glory without grief or pain?
O vision false and vain!
There lies thy cross; beneath it meekly bow;
It fits thy stature now:
Who scornful pass it with averted eye,
'Twill crush them by-and-by.

'Raise thy repining eyes, and take true measure
Of thine eternal treasure;
The Father of thy Lord can grudge thee nought,
The world for thee was bought;
And as this landscape broad - earth, sea, and sky, '
All centres in thine eye,
So all God does, if rightly understood,
Shall work thy final good.'

TWENTY-FIRST SUNDAY AFTER TRINITY

The vision is yet for an appointed time, but at the end it shall
speak, and not lie: though it tarry, wait for it, because it will
surely come, it will not tarry. Habakkuk ii. 3.

The morning mist is clear'd away,
Yet still the face of Heaven is grey,
Nor yet this autumnal breeze has stirr'd the grove,
Faded yet full, a paler green
Skirts soberly the tranquil scene,
The red-breast warbles round this leafy cove.

Sweet messenger of 'calm decay,.'
Saluting sorrow as you may,
As one still bent to find or make the best,
In thee, and in this quiet mead,
The lesson of sweet peace I read,
Rather in all to be resign'd than blest.

'Tis a low chant, according well
With the soft solitary knell,
As homeward from some grave belov'd we turn,
Or by some holy death-bed dear,
Most welcome to the chasten'd ear
Of her whom Heaven is teaching how to mourn.

O cheerful tender strain! the heart
That duly bears with you its part,
Singing so thankful to the dreary blast,
Though gone and spent its joyous prime,
And on the world's autumnal time,
'Mid wither'd hues and sere, its lot be cast:

That is the heart for thoughtful seer,
Watching, in trance nor dark nor clear, [96]
Th' appalling Future as it nearer draws:
His spirit calm'd the storm to meet,
Feeling the rock beneath his feet,
And tracing through the cloud th' eternal Cause.

That is the heart for watchman true
Waiting to see what GOD will do,
As o'er the Church the gathering twilight falls
No more he strains his wistful eye,
If chance the golden hours be nigh,
By youthful Hope seen beaming round her walls.

Forc'd from his shadowy paradise,
His thoughts to Heaven the steadier rise:
There seek his answer when the world reproves:
Contented in his darkling round,
If only he be faithful found,
When from the east the eternal morning moves.

Note: The expression, 'calm delay,' is borrowed from a friend -
by whose
kind permission the following stanzas are here inserted.
TO THE RED-BREAST.

Unheard in summer's flaring ray,
Pour forth thy notes, sweet singer,
Wooing the stillness of the autumn day:
Bid it a moment linger,

Nor fly
Too soon from winter's scowling eye.

The blackbird's song at even-tide,
And hers, who gay ascends,
Filling the heavens far and wide,
Are sweet. But none so blends,
As thine,
With calm decay, and peace divine.

[96] It shall come to pass in that day, that the light shall not be clear, nor dark. Zechariah xiv. 5.

TWENTY-SECOND SUNDAY AFTER TRINITY

Lord, how oft shall my brother sin against me, and I forgive
him? St.Matthew xviii. 21.

What liberty so glad and gay,
As where the mountain boy,
Reckless of regions far away,
A prisoner lives in joy?

The dreary sounds of crowded earth,
The cries of camp or town,
Never untun'd his lonely mirth,
Nor drew his visions down.

The snow-clad peaks of rosy light
That meet his morning view,
The thwarting cliffs that bound his sight,
They bound his fancy too.

Two ways alone his roving eye
For aye may onward go,
Or in the azure deep on high,
Or darksome mere below.

O blest restraint! more blessed range!
Too soon the happy child

His nook of homely thought will change
For life's seducing wild:

Too soon his alter'd day-dreams show
This earth a boundless space,
With sun-bright pleasures to and fro
Sporting in joyous race:

While of his narrowing heart each year,
Heaven less and less will fill,
Less keenly, thorough his grosser ear,
The tones of mercy thrill.

It must be so: else wherefore falls
The Saviour's voice unheard,
While from His pard'ning Cross He calls,
'O spare as I have spar'd?'

By our own niggard rule we try
The hope to suppliants given!
We mete out love, as if our eye
Saw to the end of Heaven.

Yes, ransom'd sinner! wouldst thou know
How often to forgive,
How dearly to embrace thy foe,
Look where thou hop'st to live; -

When thou hast told those isles of light,
And fancied all beyond,
Whatever owns, in depth or height,
Creation's wondrous bond;

Then in their solemn pageant learn
Sweet mercy's praise to see:
Their Lord resign'd them all, to earn
The bliss of pardoning thee.

TWENTY-THIRD SUNDAY AFTER TRINITY

Who shall change our vile body, that it may be fashioned like
unto His glorious body, according to the working whereby He is
able even to subdue all things onto Himself. Philippians iii. 21.

Red o'er the forest peers the setting sun,
The line of yellow light dies fast away
That crown'd the eastern copse: and chill and dun
Falls on the moor the brief November day.

Now the tir'd hunter winds a parting note,
And Echo hide good-night from every glade;
Yet wait awhile, and see the calm heaves float
Each to his rest beneath their parent shade.

How like decaying life they seem to glide!
And yet no second spring have they in store,
But where they fall, forgotten to abide
Is all their portion, and they ask no more.

Soon o'er their heads blithe April airs shall sing,
A thousand wild-flowers round them shall unfold,
The green buds glisten in the dews of Spring,
And all be vernal rapture as of old.

Unconscious they in waste oblivion lie,

In all the world of busy life around
No thought of them; in all the bounteous sky,
No drop, for them, of kindly influence found.

Man's portion is to die and rise again '
Yet he complains, while these unmurmuring part
With their sweet lives, as pure from sin and stain,
As his when Eden held his virgin heart.

And haply half unblam'd his murmuring voice
Might sound in Heaven, were all his second life
Only the first renew'd - the heathen's choice,
A round of listless joy and weary strife.

For dreary were this earth, if earth were all,
Tho' brighten'd oft by dear Affection's kiss; -
Who for the spangles wears the funeral pall?
But catch a gleam beyond it, and 'tis bliss.

Heavy and dull this frame of limbs and heart,
Whether slow creeping on cold earth, or borne
On lofty steed, or loftier prow, we dart
O'er wave or field: yet breezes laugh to scorn

Our puny speed, and birds, and clouds in heaven,
And fish, living shafts that pierce the main,
And stars that shoot through freezing air at even '
Who but would follow, might he break his chain?

And thou shalt break it soon; the grovelling worm
Shall find his wings, and soar as fast and free
As his transfigur'd Lord with lightning form
And snowy vest - such grace He won for thee,

When from the grave He sprang at dawn of morn,
And led through boundless air thy conquering road,
Leaving a glorious track, where saints, new-born,

Might fearless follow to their blest abode.

But first, by many a stern and fiery blast
The world's rude furnace must thy blood refine,
And many a gale of keenest woe be pass'd,
Till every pulse beat true to airs divine,

Till every limb obey the mounting soul,
The mounting soul, the call by Jesus given.
He who the stormy heart can so control,
The laggard body soon will waft to Heaven.

TWENTY-FOURTH SUNDAY AFTER TRINITY

The heart knoweth his own bitterness: and a stranger doth not
intermeddle with his joy. Proverbs xiv. 10.

Why should we faint and fear to live alone,
Since all alone, so Heaven has will'd, we die, [97]
Nor e'en the tenderest heart, and next our own,
Knows half the reasons why we smile and sigh?

Each in his hidden sphere of joy or woe
Our hermit spirits dwell, and range apart,
Our eyes see all around in gloom or glow '
Hues of their own, fresh borrow'd from the heart.

And well it is for us our God should feel
Alone our secret throbbings: so our prayer
May readier spring to Heaven, nor spend its zeal
On cloud-born idols of this lower air.

For if one heart in perfect sympathy
Beat with another, answering love for love,
Weak mortals, all entranc'd, on earth would lie,
Nor listen for those purer strains above.

Or what if Heaven for once its searching light
Lent to some partial eye, disclosing all

The rude bad thoughts, that in our bosom's night
Wander at large, nor heed Love's gentle thrall?

Who would not shun the dreary uncouth place?
As if, fond leaning where her infant slept,
A mother's arm a serpent should embrace:
So might we friendless live, and die unwept.

Then keep the softening veil in mercy drawn,
Thou who canst love us, thro' Thou read us true;
As on the bosom of th' aerial lawn
Melts in dim haze each coarse ungentle hue.

So too may soothing Hope Thy heave enjoy
Sweet visions of long-sever'd hearts to frame:
Though absence may impair, or cares annoy,
Some constant mind may draw us still the same.

We in dark dreams are tossing to and fro,
Pine with regret, or sicken with despair,
The while she bathes us in her own chaste glow,
And with our memory wings her own fond prayer.

O bliss of child-like innocence, and love
Tried to old age! creative power to win,
And raise new worlds, where happy fancies rove,
Forgetting quite this grosser world of sin.

Bright are their dreams, because their thoughts are clear,
Their memory cheering: but th' earth-stained spright,
Whose wakeful musings are of guilt and fear,
Must hover nearer earth, and less in light.

Farewell, for her, th' ideal scenes so fair '
Yet not farewell her hope, since thou hast deign'd,
Creator of all hearts! to own and share
The woe of what Thou mad'st, and we have stain'd.

KEBLE

Thou knowst our bitterness - our joys are Thine [98] '
No stranger Thou to all our wanderings wild:
Nor could we bear to think, how every line
Of us, Thy darken'd likeness and defil'd,

Stands in full sunshine of Thy piercing eye,
But that Thou call'st us Brethren: sweet repose
Is in that word - the Lord who dwells on high
Knows all, yet loves us better than He knows.

[97] Je mourrai seul. Pascal.
[98] Thou hast known my soul in adversities. Psalm xxxi. 7.

TWENTY-FIFTH SUNDAY AFTER TRINITY

The hoary head is a crown of glory, if it be found in the way of righteousness. Proverbs xvi. 31.

The bright-hair'd morn is glowing
O'er emerald meadows gay,
With many a clear gem strewing
The early shepherd's way.
Ye gentle elves, by Fancy seen
Stealing away with night
To slumber in your leafy screen,
Tread more than airy light.

And see what joyous greeting
The sun through heaven has shed,
Though fast yon shower be fleeting,
His beams have faster sped.
For lo! above the western haze
High towers the rainbow arch
In solid span of purest rays:
How stately is its march!

Pride of the dewy morning!
The swain's experienc'd eye
From thee takes timely warning,
Nor trusts the gorgeous sky.

For well he knows, such dawnings gay
Bring noons of storm and shower,
And travellers linger on the way
Beside the sheltering bower.

E'en so, in hope and trembling
Should watchful shepherd view
His little lambs assembling,
With glance both kind and true;
'Tis not the eye of keenest blaze,
Nor the quick-swelling breast,
That soonest thrills at touch of praise '
These do not please him best.

But voices low and gentle,
And timid glances shy,
That seem for aid parental
To sue all wistfully,
Still pressing, longing to be right,
Yet fearing to be wrong, '
In these the Pastor dares delight,
A lamb-like, Christ-like throng.

These in Life's distant even
Shall shine serenely bright,
As in th' autumnal heaven
Mild rainbow tints at night,
When the last shower is stealing down,
And ere they sink to rest,
The sun-beams weave a parting crown
For some sweet woodland nest.

The promise of the morrow
Is glorious on that eve,
Dear as the holy sorrow
When good men cease to live.
When brightening ere it die away

Mounts up their altar flame,
Still tending with intenser ray
To Heaven whence first it came.

Say not it dies, that glory,
'Tis caught unquench'd on high,
Those saintlike brows so hoary
Shall wear it in the sky.
No smile is like the smile of death,
When all good musings past
Rise wafted with the parting breath,
The sweetest thought the last.

SUNDAY NEXT BEFORE ADVENT

Gather up the fragments that remain, that nothing be lost. St. John vi. 12.

Will God indeed with fragments bear,
Snatch'd late from the decaying year?
Or can the Saviour's blood endear
The dregs of a polluted life?
When down th' o'erwhelming current tost
Just ere he sink for ever lost,
The sailor's untried arms are cross'd
In agonizing prayer, will Ocean cease her strife?

Sighs that exhaust but not relieve
Heart-rending sighs, O spare to heave
A bosom freshly taught to grieve
For lavish'd hours and love misspent!
Now through her round of holy thought
The Church our annual steps has brought,
But we no holy fire have caught '
Back on the gaudy world our wilful eyes were bent.

Too soon th' ennobling carols, pour'd
To hymn the birth-night of the Lord,
Which duteous Memory should have stor'd
For thankful echoing all the year '
Too soon those airs have pass'd away;
Nor long within the heart would stay

THE CHRISTIAN YEAR

The silence of Christ'S dying day,
Profan'd by worldly mirth, or scar'd by worldly fear.

Some strain of hope and victory
On Easter wings might lift us high
A little while we sought the sky:
And when the Spirit'S beacon fires
On every hill began to blare,
Lightening the world with glad amaze,
Who but must kindle while they gaze?
But faster than she soars, our earth-bound Fancy tires.

Nor yet for these, nor all the rites,
By which our Mother's voice invites
Our God to bless our home delights,
And sweeten every secret tear: '
The funeral dirge, the marriage vow,
The hollow'd font where parents bow,
And now elate and trembling now
To the Redeemer's feet their new-found treasures bear: '

Not for this Pastor's gracious arm
Stretch'd out to bless - a Christian charm
To dull the shafts of worldly harm: '
Nor, sweetest, holiest, best of all
For the dear feast of Jesus dying,
Upon that altar ever lying,
Where souls with sacred hunger sighing
Are call'd to sit and eat, while angels prostrate fall: '

No, not for each and all of these,
Have our frail spirits found their ease.
The gale that stirs the autumnal trees
Seems tun'd as truly to our hearts
As when, twelve weary months ago,
'Twas moaning bleak, so high and low,
You would have thought Remorse and Woe

Had taught the innocent air their sadly thrilling parts.

Is it, Christ's light is too divine,
We dare not hope like Him to shine?
But see, around His dazzling shrine
Earths gems the fire of Heaven have caught;
Martyrs and saints - each glorious day
Dawning in order on our way '
Remind us, how our darksome clay
May keep th' ethereal warmth our new Creator brought.

These we have scorn'd, O false and frail!
And now once more th' appalling tale,
How love divine may woo and fail,
Of our lost year in Heaven is told '
What if as far our life were past,
Our weeks all number'd to the last,
With time and hope behind us cast,
And all our work to do with palsied hands and cold?

O watch and pray ere Advent dawn!
For thinner than the subtlest lawn
'Twixt thee and death the veil is drawn.
But Love too late can never glow:
The scatter'd fragments Love can glean
Refine the dregs, and yield us clean
To regions where one thought serene
Breathes sweeter than whole years of sacrifice below.

ST. ANDREW'S DAY

He first findeth his own brother Simon, and saith unto him, We
have found the Messias . . . And he brought him to Jesus.
St. John i. 41, 42.

When brothers part for manhood's race,
What gift may most endearing prove
To keep fond memory its her place,
And certify a brother's love?

'Tis true, bright hours together told,
And blissful dreams in secret shar'd,
Serene or solemn, gay or bold,
Shall last in fancy unimpair'd.

E'en round the death-bed of the good
Such dear remembrances will hover,
And haunt us with no vexing mood
When all the cares of earth are over.

But yet our craving spirits feel,
We shall live on, though Fancy die,
And seek a surer pledge - a seal
Of love to last eternally.

Who art thou, that wouldst grave thy name
Thus deeply in a brother's heart?
Look on this saint, and learn to frame

Thy love-charm with true Christian art.

First seek thy Saviour out, and dwell
Beneath this shadow of His roof,
Till thou have scann'd His features well,
And known Him for the Christ by proof;

Such proof as they are sure to find
Who spend with Him their happy days,
Clean hands, and a self-ruling mind
Ever in tune for love and praise.

Then, potent with the spell of Heaven,
Go, and thine erring brother gain,
Entice him home to be forgiven,
Till he, too, see his Saviour plain.

Or, if before thee in the race,
Urge him with thine advancing tread,
Till, like twin stars, with even pace,
Each lucid course be duly aped.

No fading frail memorial give
To soothe his soul when thou art gone,
But wreaths of hope for aye to live,
And thoughts of good together done.

That so, before the judgment-seat,
Though chang'd and glorified each face,
Not unremember'd ye may meet
For endless ages to embrace.

ST. THOMAS' DAY

Thomas, because thou hast seen Me, thou hast believed; blessed
are they that have not seen, and yet have believed.
St. John xx. 29.

We were not by when Jesus came, [99]
But round us, far and near,
We see His trophies, and His name
In choral echoes hear.
In a fair ground our lot is cast,
As in the solemn week that past,
While some might doubt, but all ador'd, [100]
Ere the whole widow'd Church had seen her risen Lord.

Slowly, as then, His bounteous hand
The golden chain unwinds,
Drawing to Heaven with gentlest band
Wise hearts and loving minds.
Love sought Him first - at dawn of morn [101]
From her sad couch she sprang forlorn,
She sought to weep with Thee alone,
And saw Thine open grave, and knew that thou wert gone.

Reason and Faith at once set out [102]
To search the Saviour'S tomb;
Faith faster runs, but waits without,
As fearing to presume,
Till Reason enter in, and trace

Christ's relics round the holy place '
'Here lay His limbs, and here His sacred head,
And who was by, to make His new-forsaken bed?'

Both wonder, one believes - but while
They muse on all at home,
No thought can tender Love beguile
From Jesus' grave to roam.
Weeping she stays till He appear '
Her witness first the Church must hear '
All joy to souls that can rejoice
With her at earliest call of His dear gracious voice.

Joy too to those, who love to talk
In secret how He died,
Though with seal'd eyes awhile they walk,
Nor see him at their side:
Most like the faithful pair are they,
Who once to Emmaus took their way,
Half darkling, till their Master shied
His glory on their souls, made known in breaking bread.

Thus, ever brighter and more bright,
On those He came to save
The Lord of new-created light
Dawn'd gradual from the grave;
Till pass'd th' enquiring day-light hour,
And with clos'd door in silent bower
The Church in anxious musing sate,
As one who for redemption still had long to wait.

Then, gliding through th' unopening door,
Smooth without step or sound,
'Peace to your souls,' He said - no more '
They own Him, kneeling round.
Eye, ear, and hand, and loving heart,
Body and soul in every part,

Successive made His witnesses that hour,
Cease not in all the world to show His saving power.

Is there, on earth, a spirit frail,
Who fears to take their word,
Scarce daring, through the twilight pale,
To think he sees the Lord?
With eyes too tremblingly awake
To bear with dimness for His sake?
Read and confess the Hand Divine
That drew thy likeness here so true in every line.

For all thy rankling doubts so sore,
Love thou thy Saviour still,
Him for thy Lord and God adore,
And ever do His will.
Though vexing thoughts may seem to last,
Let not thy soul be quite o'ercast; -
Soon will He show thee all His wounds, and say,
'Long have I known Thy name [103] - know thou My face alway.'

[99] Thomas, one of the twelve, called Didymus, was not with them when Jesus came. St. John xx. 24.
[100] When they saw Him, they worshipped Him; but some doubted. St. Matthew xxviii. 17.
[101] St. Mary Magdalene's visit to the sepulchre.
[102] St. Peter and St. John.
[103] In Exodus xxxiii. 17, God says to Moses, 'I know thee by name;' meaning, 'I bear especial favour towards thee.' Thus our Savious speaks to St. Thomas by name in the place here referred to.

THE CONVERSION OF ST. PAUL

And he fell to the earth, and heard a voice saying unto him, Saul,
Saul, why persecutest thou Me? And he said, Who art Thou,
Lord? And the Lord said, I am Jesus whom thou persecutest.
Acts ix. 4, 5.

The midday sun, with fiercest glare,
Broods o'er the hazy twinkling air:
Along the level sand
The palm-tree's shade unwavering lies,
Just as thy towers, Damascus, rise
To greet you wearied band.

The leader of that martial crew
Seems bent some mighty deed to do,
So steadily he speeds,
With lips firm clos'd and fixed eye,
Like warrior when the fight is night,
Nor talk nor landscape heeds.

What sudden blaze is round him pour'd,
As though all Heaven's refulgent hoard
In one rich glory shone?
One moment - and to earth he falls:
What voice his inmost heart appalls? '
Voice heard by him alone.

For to the rest both words and form

Seem lost in lightning and in storm,
While Saul, in wakeful trance,
Sees deep within that dazzling field
His persecuted Lord reveal'd,
With keen yet pitying glance:

And hears time meek upbraiding call
As gently on his spirit fall,
As if th' Almighty Son
Were prisoner yet in this dark earth,
Nor had proclaim'd His royal birth,
Nor His great power begun.

'Ah! wherefore persecut'st thou Me?'
He heard and saw, and sought to free
His strain'd eyes from the sight:
But Heaven's high magic bound it there,
Still gazing, though untaught to bear
Th' insufferable light.

'Who art Thou, Lord?' he falters forth: '
So shall Sin ask of heaven and earth
At the last awful day.
'When did we see Thee suffering nigh, [104]
And pass'd Thee with unheeding eye?
Great God of judgment, say!'

Ah! little dream our listless eyes
What glorious presence they despise,
While, in our noon of life,
To power or fame we rudely press. '
Christ is at hand, to scorn or bless,
Christ suffers in our strife.

And though heaven's gate long since have clos'd,
And our dear Lord in bliss repos'd,
High above mortal ken,

To every ear in every land
(Thought meek ears only understand)
He speaks as he did then.

'Ah! wherefore persecute ye Me?
'Tis hard, ye so in love should be
With your own endless woe.
Know, though at God's right hand I live,
I feel each wound ye reckless give
To the least saint below.

'I in your care My brethren left,
Not willing ye should be bereft
Of waiting on your Lord.
The meanest offering ye can make '
A drop of water - for love's sake, [105]
In Heaven, be sure, is stor'd.'

O by those gentle tones and dear,
When thou hast stay'd our wild career,
Thou only hope of souls,
Ne'er let us cast one look behind,
But in the thought of Jesus find
What every thought controls.

As to Thy last Apostle's heart
Thy lightning glance did then impart
Zeal's never-dying fire,
So teach us on Thy shrine to lay
Our hearts, and let them day by day
Intenser blaze and higher.

And as each mild and winning note
(Like pulses that round harp-strings float
When the full strain is o'er)
Left lingering on his inward ear
Music, that taught, as death drew near,

Love's lesson more and more:

So, as we walk our earthly round,
Still may the echo of that sound
Be in our memory stor'd
'Christians! behold your happy state:
Christ is in these, who round you wait;
Make much of your dear Lord!'

[104] St. Mathew xxv. 44.
[105] St. Matthew x. 42.

THE PURIFICATION

Blessed are the pure in heart: for they shall see God.
St. Matthew v. 8.

Bless'd are the pure in heart,
For they shall see our God,
The secret of the Lord is theirs,
Their soul is Christ's abode.

Might mortal thought presume
To guess an angel's lay,
Such are the notes that echo through
The courts of Heaven to-day.

Such the triumphal hymns
On Sion's Prince that wait,
In high procession passing on
Towards His temple-gate.

Give ear, ye kings - bow down,
Ye rulers of the earth '
This, this is He: your Priest by grace,
Your God and King by birth.

No pomp of earthly guards
Attends with sword and spear,
And all-defying, dauntless look,
Their monarch's way to clear;

Yet are there more with Him
Than all that are with you '
The armies of the highest Heaven,
All righteous, good, and true.

Spotless their robes and pure,
Dipp'd in the sea of light,
That hides the unapproached shrine
From men's and angels' sight.

His throne, thy bosom blest,
O mother undefil'd '
That throne, if aught beneath the skies,
Beseems the sinless child.

Lost in high thoughts, 'whose son
The wondrous Babe might prove,'
Her guileless husband walks beside,
Bearing the hallow'd dove;

Meet emblem of His vow,
Who, on this happy day,
His dove-like soul - best sacrifice '
Did on God's altar lay.

But who is he, by years
Bow'd, but erect in heart,
Whose prayers are struggling with his tears?
'Lord, let me now depart.

'Now hath Thy servant seen
Thy saving health, O Lord;
'Tis time that I depart in peace,
According to Thy word.'

Yet swells this pomp: one more

Comes forth to bless her God;
Full fourscore years, meek widow, she
Her heaven-ward way hath troth.

She who to earthly joys
So long had given farewell,
Now sees, unlook'd for, Heaven on earth,
Christ in His Israel.

Wide open from that hour
The temple-gates are set,
And still the saints rejoicing there
The holy Child have met.

Now count His train to-day,
Auth who may meet Him, learn:
Him child-like sires, meek maidens find,
Where pride can nought discern.

Still to the lowly soul
He doth Himself impart,
And for His cradle and His throne
Chooseth the pure in heart.

ST. MATTHIAS' DAY

Wherefore of these men which have companied with us all the time that the Lord Jesus went in and out among us, beginning from the baptism of John, unto the same day that He was taken up from us, must one be ordained to be a witness with us of His resurrection. Acts i. 21, 22.

Who is God's chosen priest?
He, who on Christ stands waiting day and night,
Who trac'd His holy steps, nor ever ceas'd,
From Jordan banks to Bethphage height:

Who hath learn'd lowliness
From his Lord's cradle, patience from His Cross;
Whom poor men's eyes and hearts consent to bless;
To whom, for Christ, the world is loss;

Who both in agony
Hath seen Him and in glory; and in both
Own'd Him divine, and yielded, nothing loth,
Body and soul, to live and die,

In witness of his Lord,
In humble following of his Saviour dear:
This is the man to wield th' unearthly sword,
Warring unharm'd with sin and fear.

But who can o'er suffice '

What mortal - for this more than angels' task,
Winning or losing souls, Thy life-blood's price?
The gift were too divine to ask.

But Thou hast made it sure
By Thy dear promise to thy Church and Bride,
That Thou, on earth, wouldst aye with her endure,
Till earth to Heaven be purified.

Thou art her only spouse,
Whose arm supports her, on Whose faithful breast
Her persecuted head she meekly bows,
Sure pledge of her eternal rest.

Thou, her unerring guide,
Stayest her fainting steps along the wild;
Thy merit is on the bowers of lust and pride,
That she may pass them undefil'd.

Who then, uncall'd by Thee,
Dare touch Thy spouse, Thy very self below?
Or who dare count him summoned worthily,
Except Thine hand and seal he show?

Where can Thy seal be found,
But on thou chosen seed, from age to age
By thine anointed heralds duly crown'd,
As kings and priests Thy war to wage?

Then fearless walk we forth,
Yet full of trembling, Messengers of God:
Our warrant sure, but doubting of our worth,
By our own shame alike and glory aw'd.

Dread Searcher of the hearts,
Thou who didst seal by Thy descending Dove
Thy servant's choice, O help us in our parts,

Else helpless found, to learn and teach Thy love.

THE ANNUNCIATION OF THE BLESSED VIRGIN MARY

And the Angel came in unto her, and said, Hail, thou that art highly favoured, the Lord is with thee: blessed art thou among women. St. Luke i.28.

O Thou who deign'st to sympathise
With all our frail and fleshly ties,
Maker yet Brother dear,
Forgive the too presumptuous thought,
If, calming wayward grief, I sought
To gaze on Thee too near.

Yet sure 'twas not presumption, Lord,
'Twas Thine own comfortable word
That made the lesson known:
Of all the dearest bonds we prove,
Thou countest sons and mothers' love
Most sacred, most Thine own.

When wandering here a little span,
Thou took'st on Thee to rescue man,
Thou had'st no earthly sire:
That wedded love we prize so dear,
As if our heaven and home were here,
It lit in Thee no fire.

On no sweet sister's faithful breast
Wouldst Thou Thine aching forehead rest,
On no kind brother lean:
But who, O perfect filial heart,
E'er did like Thee a true son's part,
Endearing, firm, serene?

Thou wept'st, meek maiden, mother mild,
Thou wept'st upon thy sinless Child,
Thy very heart was riven:
And yet, what mourning matron here
Would deem thy sorrows bought too dear
By all on this side Heaven?

A Son that never did amiss,
That never sham'd His Mother's kiss,
Nor cross'd her fondest prayer:
Even from the tree He deign'd to bow,
For her His agonised brow,
Her, His sole earthly care.

Ave Maria! blessed Maid!
Lily of Eden's fragrant shade,
Who can express the love
That nurtur'd thee so pure and sweet,
Making thy heart a shelter meet
For Jesus' holy dove?

Ave Maria! Mother blest,
To whom, caressing and caress'd,
Clings the eternal Child;
Favour'd beyond Archangels' dream,
When first on Thee with tenderest gleam
Thy new-born Saviour smil'd: '

Ave Maria! thou whose name
All but adoring love may claim,

247

Yet may we reach thy shrine;
For He, thy Son and Saviour, vows
To crown all lowly lofty brows
With love and joy like thine.

Bless'd is the womb that bare Him - bless'd [106]
The bosom where His lips were press'd,
But rather bless'd are they
Who hear His word and keep it well,
The living homes where Christ shall dwell,
And never pass away.

[106] St. Luke xi. 27, 28.

ST. MARK'S DAY

And the contention was so sharp between them, that they departed asunder one from the other. Acts xv. 30. Compare 2 Tim. iv. 11. Take Mark, and bring him with thee: for he is profitable to me for the ministry.

Oh! who shall dare in this frail scene
On holiest happiest thoughts to lean,
On Friendship, Kindred, or on Love?
Since not Apostles' hands can clasp
Each other in so firm a grasp
But they shall change and variance prove.

Yet deem not, on such parting sad
Shall dawn no welcome dear and glad:
Divided in their earthly race,
Together at the glorious goal,
Each leading many a rescu'd soul,
The faithful champions shall embrace.

For e'en as those mysterious Four,
Who the bright whirling wheels upbore
By Chebar in the fiery blast. [107]
So, on their tasks of love and praise
This saints of God their several ways
Right onward speed, yet join at last.

And sometimes e'en beneath the moon

The Saviour gives a gracious boon,
When reconciled Christians meet,
And face to face, and heart to heart,
High thoughts of holy love impart
In silence meek, or converse sweet.

Companion of the Saints! 'twas thine
To taste that drop of peace divine,
When the great soldier of thy Lord
Call'd thee to take his last farewell,
Teaching the Church with joy to tell
The story of your love restor'd.

O then the glory and the bliss,
When all that pain'd or seem'd amiss
Shall melt with earth and sin away!
When saints beneath their Saviour's eye,
Fill'd with each other's company,
Shall spend in love th' eternal day!

[107] They turned not when they went; they went every one
straight onward. Ezekiel 1. 9.

ST. PHILIP AND ST. JAMES

Let the brother of low degree rejoice in that he is exalted: but the rich in that he is made low. St. James i. 9, 10.

Dear is the morning gale of spring,
And dear th' autumnal eve;
But few delights can summer bring
A Poet's crown to weave.

Her bowers are mute, her fountains dry,
And ever Fancy's wing
Speed's from beneath her cloudless sky
To autumn or to spring.

Sweet is the infant's waking smile,
And sweet the old man's rest '
But middle age by no fond wile,
No soothing calm is blest.

Still in the world's hot restless gleam
She plies her weary task,
While vainly for some pleasant dream
Her wandering glances ask. '

O shame upon thee, listless heart,
So sad a sigh to heave,
As if thy Saviour had no part
In thoughts, that make thee grieve.

As if along His lonesome way
He had not borne for thee
Sad languors through the summer day,
Storms on the wintry sea.

Youth's lightning flash of joy secure
Pass'd seldom o'er His spright, '
A well of serious thought and pure.
Too deep for earthly light.

No spring was His - no fairy gleam '
For He by trial knew
How cold and bare what mortals dream,
To worlds where all is true.

Then grudge not thou the anguish keen
Which makes thee like thy Lord,
And learn to quit with eye serene
Thy youth's ideal hoard.

Thy treasur'd hopes and raptures high '
Unmurmuring let them go,
Nor grieve the bliss should quickly fly
Which Christ disdain'd to know.

Thou shalt have joy in sadness soon;
The pure, calm hope be thine,
Which brightens, like the eastern moon,
As day's wild lights decline.

Thus souls, by nature pitch'd too high,
By sufferings plung'd too low,
Meet in the Church's middle sky,
Half way 'twixt joy and woe,

To practise there the soothing lay

THE CHRISTIAN YEAR

That sorrow best relieves;
Thankful for all God takes away,
Humbled by all He gives.

ST. BARNABAS.

The sea of consolation, a Levite. Acts iv. 36.

The world's a room of sickness, where each heart
Knows its own anguish and unrest;
The truest wisdom there, and noblest art,
Is his, who skills of comfort best;
Whom by the softest step and gentlest tone
Enfeebled spirits own,
And love to raise the languid eye,
When, like an angel's wing, they feel him fleeting by: '

Feel only - for in silence gently gliding
Fain would he shun both ear and sight,
'Twixt Prayer and watchful Love his heart dividing,
A nursing-father day and night.
Such were the tender arms, where cradled lay,
In her sweet natal day,
The Church of Jesus; such the love
He to His chosen taught for His dear widow'd Dove.

Warm'd underneath the Comforter's safe wing
They spread th' endearing warmth around:
Mourners, speed here your broken hearts to bring,
Here healing dews and balms abound:
Here are soft hands that cannot bless in vain,
By trial taught your pain:
Here loving hearts, that daily know

The heavenly consolations they on you bestow.

Sweet thoughts are theirs, that breathe serenest calms,
Of holy offerings timely paid, [108]
Of fire from heaven to bless their votive alms
And passions on God's altar laid.
The world to them is clos'd, and now they shine
With rays of love divine,
Through darkest nooks of this dull earth
Pouring, in showery times, their glow of 'quiet mirth.'

New hearts before their Saviour's feet to lay,
This is their first, their dearest joy:
Their next from heart to heart to clear the way [109]
For mutual love without alloy:
Never so blest as when in Jesus' roll
They write some hero-soul,
More pleas'd upon his brightening road
To wait, than if their own with all his radiance glow'd.

O happy spirits, mark'd by God and man
Their messages of love to bear, [110]
What though long since in Heaven your brows began,
The genial amarant wreath to wear,
And in th' eternal leisure of calm love
Ye banquet there above;
Yet in your sympathetic heart
We and our earthly griefs may ask and hope a part.

Comfort's true sons! amid the thoughts of down
That strew your pillow of repose,
Sure 'tis one joy to muse, how ye unknown
By sweet remembrance soothe our woes;
And how the spark ye lit, of heavenly cheer,
Lives in our embers here,
Where'er the cross is borne with smiles,
Or lighten'd secretly by Love's endearing wiles:

Where'er one Levite in the temple keeps
The watch-fire of his midnight prayer,
Or issuing thence, the eyes of mourners steeps
In heavenly balm, fresh gather'd there;
Thus saints, that seem to die in earth's rude strife,
Only win double life:
They have but left our weary ways
To live in memory here, in Heaven by love and praise.

[108] Having land, sold it, and brought the money, and laid it at the Apostle's feet. Acts iv. 37.
[109] Barnabas took him, and brought him (Saul) to the Apostles. Acts ix. 27.
[110] Acts xi. 22: xiii. 2.

ST. JOHN BAPTIST'S DAY

Behold, I will send you Elijah the prophet before the coming of
the great and dreadful day of the Lord: and he shall turn the heart
of the fathers to the children, and the heart of the children to
their fathers. Malachi iv. 5, 6.

Twice in her season of decay
The fallen Church hath felt Elijah's eye
Dart from the wild its piercing ray:
Not keener burns, in the chill morning sky,
The herald star,
Whose torch afar
Shadows and boding night-birds fly.

Methinks we need him once again,
That favour'd seer - but where shall he be found?
By Cherith's side we seek in vain,
In vain on Carmel's green and lonely mound:
Angels no more
From Sinai soar,
On his celestial errands bound.

But wafted to her glorious place
By harmless fire, among the ethereal thrones,
His spirit with a dear embrace
Thee the lov'd harbinger of Jesus owns,
Well-pleas'd to view
Her likeness true,

And trace, in thine, her own deep tones.

Deathless himself, he joys with thee
To commune how a faithful martyr dies,
And in the blest could envy be,
He would behold thy wounds with envious eyes,
Star of our morn,
Who yet unborn [111]
Didst guide our hope, where Christ should rise.

Now resting from your jealous care
For sinners, such as Eden cannot know,
Ye pour for us your mingled prayer,
No anxious fear to damp Affection's glow,
Love draws a cloud
From you to shroud
Rebellion's mystery here below.

And since we see, and not afar,
The twilight of the great and dreadful day,
Why linger, till Elijah's car
Stoop from the clouds? Why sheep ye? Rise and pray,
Ye heralds seal'd
In camp or field
Your Saviour's banner to display.

Where is the lore the Baptist taught,
The soul unswerving and the fearless tongue?
The much-enduring wisdom, sought
By lonely prayer the haunted rocks among?
Who counts it gain [112]
His light should wane,
So the whole world to Jesus throng?

Thou Spirit, who the Church didst lend
Her eagle wings, to shelter in the wild, [113]
We pray Thee, ere the Judge descend,

With flames like these, all bright and undefil'd,
Her watch-fires light,
To guide aright
Our weary souls by earth beguil'd.

So glorious let thy Pastors shine,
That by their speaking lives the world may learn
First filial duty, then divine, [114]
That sons to parents, all to Thee may turn;
And ready prove
In fires of love,
At sight of Thee, for aye to burn.

[111] The babe leaped in my womb for joy. St. Luke i. 44.
[112] He must increase, but I must decrease. St. John iii. 30.
[113] Revelations xii. 14.
[114] He must turn the heart of the fathers to the children, and the heart of the children to the fathers. Malachi iv. 6. To turn the hearts of the fathers to the children, and the disobedient to the wisdom of the just; to make ready a people prepared for the Lord. St. Luke i. 17.

ST. PETER'S DAY

When Herod would have brought him forth, the same night Peter
was sleeping. Acts xii. 26.

Thou thrice denied, yet thrice belov'd, [115]
  Watch by Thine own forgiven friend;
In sharpest perils faithful prov'd,
  Let his soul love Thee to the end.

The prayer is heard - else why so deep
  His slumber on the eve of death?
And wherefore smiles he in his sleep
  As one who drew celestial breath?

He loves and is belov'd again '
  Can his soul choose but be at rest?
Sorrow hath fled away, and Pain
  Dares not invade the guarded nest.

He dearly loves, and not alone:
  For his wing'd thoughts are soaring high
Where never yet frail heart was known
  To breathe its vain Affection's sigh.

He loves and weeps - but more than tears
  Have seal'd Thy welcome and his love '
One look lives in him, and endears
  Crosses and wrongs where'er he rove:

That gracious chiding look, [116] Thy call
To win him to himself and Thee,
Sweetening the sorrow of his fall
Which else were ru'd too bitterly.

E'en through the veil of sheep it shines,
The memory of that kindly glance; -
The Angel watching by, divines
And spares awhile his blissful trance.

Or haply to his native lake
His vision wafts him back, to talk
With Jesus, ere His flight He take,
As in that solemn evening walk,

When to the bosom of His friend,
The Shepherd, He whose name is Good.
Did His dear lambs and sheep commend,
Both bought and nourish'd with His blood:

Then laid on him th' inverted tree,
Which firm embrac'd with heart and arm,
Might cast o'er hope and memory,
O'er life and death, its awful charm.

With brightening heart he bears it on,
His passport through this eternal gates,
To his sweet home - so nearly won,
He seems, as by the door he waits,

The unexpressive notes to hear
Of angel song and angel motion,
Rising and falling on the ear
Like waves in Joy's unbounded ocean. '

His dream is chang'd - the Tyrant's voice

Calls to that last of glorious deeds '
But as he rises to rejoice,
Not Herod but an Angel leads.

He dreams he sees a lamp flash bright,
Glancing around his prison room '
But 'tis a gleam of heavenly light
That fills up all the ample gloom.

The flame, that in a few short years
Deep through the chambers of the dead
Shall pierce, and dry the fount of tears,
Is waving o'er his dungeon-bed.

Touch'd he upstarts - his chains unbind '
Through darksome vault, up massy stair,
His dizzy, doubting footsteps wind
To freedom and cool moonlight air.

Then all himself, all joy and calm,
Though for a while his hand forego,
Just as it touch'd, the martyr's palm,
He turns him to his task below;

The pastoral staff, the keys of Heaven,
To wield a while in grey-haired might,
Then from his cross to spring forgiven,
And follow Jesus out of sight.

[115] St. John xxi. 15-17.
[116] St. Luke xxii. 61.

ST. JAMES'S DAY

Ye shall drink indeed of My cup, and be baptised with the baptism that I am baptised with: but to sit on My right hand, and on My left, is not Mine to give, but it shall be given to them for whom it is prepared of My Father.
St. Matthew xx. 23.

Sit down and take thy fill of joy
At God's right hand, a bidden guest,
Drink of the cup that cannot cloy,
Eat of the bread that cannot waste.
O great Apostle! rightly now
Thou readest all thy Saviour meant,
What time His grave yet gentle brow
In sweet reproof on thee was bent.

'Seek ye to sit enthron'd by me?
Alas! ye know not what ye ask,
The first in shame and agony,
The lowest in the meanest task '
This can ye be? and came ye drink
The cup that I in tears must steep,
Nor from the 'whelming waters shrink
That o'er Me roll so dark and deep?'

'We can - Thine are we, dearest Lord,
In glory and in agony,
To do and suffer all Thy word;

Only be Thou for ever nigh.' '
'Then be it so - My cup receive,
And of My woes baptismal taste:
But for the crown, that angels weave
For those next Me in glory plac'd,

'I give it not by partial love;
But in My Father's book are writ
What names on earth shall lowliest prove,
That they in Heaven may highest sit.'
Take up the lesson, O my heart;
Thou Lord of meekness, write it there,
Thine own meek self to me impart,
Thy lofty hope, thy lowly prayer.

If ever on the mount with Thee
I seem to soar in vision bright,
With thoughts of coming agony, [117]
Stay Thou the too presumptuous flight:
Gently along the vale of tears
Lead me from Tabor's sunbright steep,
Let me not grudge a few short years
With thee t'ward Heaven to walk and weep:

Too happy, on my silent path,
If now and then allow'd, with Thee
Watching some placid holy death,
Thy secret work of love to see;
But, oh! most happy, should Thy call,
Thy welcome call, at last be given '
'Come where thou long hast storeth thy all
Come see thy place prepar'd in Heaven.'

[117] St. Matthew xvii. 12. 'Likewise shall also the Son of Man
suffer of them.' This was just after the Transfiguration.

ST. BARTHOLOMEW

Jesus answered and said unto him, Because I said unto thee, I saw the under the fig-tree, believest thou? Thou shalt see greater things than these. St. John i. 50.

Hold up thy mirror to the sun,
And thou shalt need an eagle's gaze,
So perfectly the polish'd stone
Gives back the glory of his rays:

Turn it, and it shall paint as true
The soft green of the vernal earth,
And each small flower of bashful hue,
That closest hides its lowly birth.

Our mirror is a blessed book,
Where out from each illumin'd page
We see one glorious Image look
All eyes to dazzle and engage,

The Son of God: and that indeed
We see Him as He is, we know,
Since in the same bright glass we read
The very life of things below. '

Eye of God's word! [118] where'er we turn
Ever upon us! thy keen gaze
Can all the depths of sin discern,

Unravel every bosom's maze:

Who that has felt thy glance of dread
Thrill through his heart's remotest cells,
About his path, about his bed,
Can doubt what spirit in thee dwells?

'What word is this? Whence know'st thou me?'
All wondering cries the humbled heart,
To hear thee that deep mystery,
The knowledge of itself, impart.

The veil is rais'd; who runs may read,
By its own light the truth is seen,
And soon the Israelite indeed
Bows down t' adore the Nazarene.

So did Nathanael, guileless man,
At once, not shame-fac'd or afraid,
Owning Him God, who so could scan
His musings in the lonely shade;

In his own pleasant fig-tree's shade,
Which by his household fountain grew,
Where at noon-day his prayer he made
To know God better than he knew.

Oh! happy hours of heavenward thought!
How richly crown'd! how well improv'd!
In musing o'er the Law he taught,
In waiting for the Lord he lov'd.

We must not mar with earthly praise
What God's approving word hath seal'd:
Enough, if might our feeble lays
Take up the promise He reveal'd;

'The child-like faith, that asks not sight,
Waits not for wonder or for sign,
Believes, because it loves, aright '
Shall see things greater, things divine.

'Heaven to that gaze shall open wide,
And brightest angels to and fro
On messages of love shall glide
'Twixt God above and Christ below.'

So still the guileless man is blest,
To him all crooked paths are straight,
Him on his way to endless rest
Fresh, ever-growing strengths await. [119]

God's witnesses, a glorious host,
Compass him daily like a cloud;
Martyrs and seers, the sav'd and lost,
Mercies and judgments cry aloud.

Yet shall to him the still small voice,
That first into his bosom found
A way, and fix'd his wavering choice,
Nearest and dearest ever sound.

[118] 'The position before us is, that we ourselves, and such as
we, are the very person who Scripture speaks of: and to whom,
as men, in every variety of persuasive form, it makes its conde-
scending though celestial appeal. The point worthy of
observation is, to note how a book of the description and the
compass which we have represented Scripture to be, possesses
this versatility of power; this eye, like that of a portrait, uni-
formly fixed upon us, turn where we will.' Miller's Bampton
Lectures, p. 128.
[119] They go from strength to strength. Psalm lxxxiv. 7.

ST. MATTHEW

And after these things He went forth, and saw a publican, named
Levi, sitting at the receipt of custom: and He said unto him, Fol-
low Me. And he left all, rose up, and followed Him.
St. Luke v. 27, 28.

Ye hermits blest, ye holy maids,
The nearest Heaven on earth,
Who talk with God in shadowy glades,
Free from rude care and mirth;
To whom some viewless teacher brings
The secret lore of rural things,
The moral of each fleeting cloud and gale,
The whispers from above, that haunt the twilight vale:

Say, when in pity ye have gaz'd
On the wreath'd smoke afar,
That o'er some town, like mist uprais'd,
Hung hiding sun and star,
Then as ye turn'd your weary eye
To the green earth and open sky,
Were ye not fain to doubt how Faith could dwell
Amid that dreary glare, in this world's citadel?

But Love's a flower that will not die
For lack of leafy screen,
And Christian Hope can cheer the eye
That ne'er saw vernal green;

Then be ye sure that Love can bless
E'en in this crowded loneliness,
Where ever-moving myriads seem to say,
Go - thou art naught to us, nor we to thee - away!

There are in this loud stunning tide
Of human care and crime,
With whom the melodies abide
Of th' everlasting chime;
Who carry music in their heart
Through dusky lane and wrangling mart,
Plying their daily task with busier feet,
Because their secret souls a holy strain repeat.

How sweet to them, in such brief rest
As thronging cares afford,
In thought to wander, fancy-blest,
To where their gracious Lord,
In vain, to win proud Pharisees,
Spake, and was heard by fell disease [120] '
But not in vain, beside yon breezy lake,
Bade the meek Publican his gainful seat forsake:

At once he rose, and left his gold;
His treasure and his heart
Transferr'd, where he shall safe behold
Earth and her idols part;
While he beside his endless store
Shall sit, and floods unceasing pour
Of Christ's true riches o'er all time and space,
First angel of His Church, first steward of His Grace.

Nor can ye not delight to think [121]
Where He vouchsaf'd to eat,
How the Most Holy did not shrink
From touch of sinner's meat;
What worldly hearts and hearts impure

269

Went with Him through the rich man's door,
That we might learn of Him lost souls to love,
And view His least and worst with hope to meet above.

These gracious lines shed Gospel light
On Mammon's gloomiest cells,
As on some city's cheerless night
The tide of sunrise swells,
Till tower, and dome, and bridge-way proud
Are mantled with a golden cloud,
And to wise hearts this certain hope us given;
'No mist that man may raise, shall hide the eye of Heaven.'

And oh! if e'en on Babel shine
Such gleams of Paradise,
Should not their peace be peace divine,
Who day by day arise
To look on clearer heavens, and scan
The work of God untouch'd by man?
Shame on us, who about us Babel bear,
And live in Paradise, as if God was not there!

[120] It seems from St. Matthew ix. 8, 9, that the calling of Levi took place immediately after the healing of the paralytic in the presence of the Pharisees.
[121] St. Matthew ix. 10.

ST. MICHAEL AND ALL ANGELS.

Are they not all ministering spirits, sent forth to minister for
them who shall be heirs of salvation?
Hebrews i. 14.

Ye stars that round the Sun of righteousness
In glorious order roll,
With harps for ever strung, ready to bless
God for each rescued soul,
Ye eagle spirits, that build in light divine,
Oh! think of us to-day,
Faint warblers of this earth, that would combine
Our trembling notes with your accepted lay.

Your amarant wreaths were earn'd; and homeward all,
Flush'd with victorious might,
Ye might have sped to keep high festival,
And revel in the light;
But meeting us, weak worldlings, on our way,
Tired ere the fight begun,
Ye turn'd to help us in th' unequal fray,
Remembering Whose we were, how dearly won:

Remembering Bethlehem, and that glorious night
When ye, who used to soar
Diverse along all space in fiery flight,
Came thronging to adore
Your God new-born, and made a sinner's child;
As if the stars should leave

Their stations in the far ethereal wild,
And round the sun a radiant circle weave.

Nor less your lay of triumph greeted fair
Our Champion and your King,
In that first strife, whence Satan in despair
Sunk down on scathed wing:
Abuse He fasted, and alone He fought;
But when His toils were o'er,
Ye to the sacred Hermit duteous brought
Banquet and hymn, your Eden's festal store.

Ye too, when lowest in th' abyss of woe
He plung'd to save His sheep,
Were leaning from your golden thrones to know
The secrets of that deep:
But clouds were on His sorrow: one alone
His agonising call
Summon'd from Heaven, to still that bitterest groan,
And comfort Him, the Comforter of all.

Oh! highest favour'd of all Spirits create
(If right of thee we deem),
How didst thou glide on brightening wing elate
To meet th' unclouded beam
Of Jesus from the couch of darkness rising!
How swell'd thine anthem's sound,
With fear and mightier joy weak hearts surprising,
'Your God is risen, and may not here be found!'

Pass a few days, and this dull darkling globe
Must yield Him from her sight; -
Brighter and brighter streams His glory-robe,
And He is lost in light.
Then, when through yonder everlasting arch,
Ye in innumerous choir
Pour'd, heralding Messiah's conquering march,

Linger'd around His skirts two forms of fire:

With us they stay'd, high warning to impart;
    'The Christ shall come again
E'en as He goes; with the same human heart,
    With the same godlike train.' '
Oh! jealous God! how could a sinner dare
    Think on that dreadful day,
But that with all Thy wounds Thou wilt be there,
And all our angel friends to bring Thee on Thy way?

Since to Thy little ones is given such grace,
    That they who nearest stand
Alway to God in Heaven, and see His face,
    Go forth at His command,
To wait around our path in weal or woe,
    As erst upon our King,
Set Thy baptismal seal upon our brow,
And waft us heavenward with enfolding wing:

Grant, Lord, that when around th' expiring world
    Our seraph guardians wait,
While on her death-bed, ere to ruin hurl'd,
    She owns Thee, all too late,
They to their charge may turn, and thankful see
    Thy mark upon us still;
Then all together rise, and reign with Thee,
And all their holy joy o'er contrite hearts fulfil!

ST. LUKE

Luke, the beloved physician, and Demas, greet you. Colossians
iv. 14. Demas hath forsaken me, having loved this present world
. . . Only Luke is with me. 2 Timothy iv. 10, 11.

Two clouds before the summer gale
In equal race fleet o'er the sky:
Two flowers, when wintry blasts assail,
Together pins, together die.

But two capricious human hearts '
No sage's rod may track their ways.
No eye pursue their lawless starts
Along their wild self-chosen maze.

He only, by whose sovereign hand
Even sinners for the evil day [122]
Were made - who rules the world He plann'd,
Turning our worst His own good way;

He only can the cause reveal,
Why, at the same fond bosom fed,
Taught in the self-same lap to kneel
Till the same prayer were duly said,

Brothers in blood and nurture too,
Aliens in heart so oft should prove;

One lose, the other keep, Heaven's clue;
One dwell in wrath, and one in love.

He only knows - for He can read
The mystery of the wicked heart '
Why vainly oft our arrows speed
When aim'd with most unerring art;

While from some rude and powerless arm
A random shaft in season sent
Shall light upon some lurking harm,
And work some wonder little meant.

Doubt we, how souls so wanton change,
Leaving their own experienc'd rest?
Need not around the world to range;
One narrow cell may teach us best.

Look in, and see Christ's chosen saint
In triumph wear his Christ-like chain;
No fear lest he should swerve or faint;
'His life is Christ, his death is gain.' [123]

Two converts, watching by his side,
Alike his love and greetings share;
Luke the belov'd, the sick soul's guide,
And Demas, nam'd in faltering prayer.

Pass a few years - look in once more '
The saint is in his bonds again;
Save that his hopes more boldly soar, [124]
He and his lot unchang'd remain.

But only Luke is with him now:
Alas! that e'en the martyr's cell,
Heaven's very gate, should scope allow
For the false world's seducing spell.

'Tis sad - but yet 'tis well, be sure,
We on the sight should muse awhile,
Nor deem our shelter all secure
Even in the Church's holiest aisle.

Vainly before the shrine he bends,
Who knows not the true pilgrim's part:
The martyr's cell no safety lends
To him who wants the martyr's heart.

But if there be, who follows Paul
As Paul his Lord, in life and death,
Where'er an aching heart may call,
Ready to speed and take no breath;

Whose joy is, to the wandering sheep
To tell of the great Shepherd's love; [125]
To learn of mourners while they weep
The music that makes mirth above;

Who makes the Saviour all his theme,
The Gospel all his pride and praise '
Approach: for thou canst feel the gleam
That round the martyr's death-bed plays:

Thou hast an ear for angels' songs,
A breath the gospel trump to fill,
And taught by thee the Church prolongs
Her hymns of high thanksgiving still. [126]

Ah! dearest mother, since too oft
The world yet wins some Demas frail
E'en from thine arms, so kind and soft,
May thy tried comforts never fail!

When faithless ones forsake thy wing,

Be it vouchsaf'd thee still to see
Thy true, fond nurslings closer cling,
Cling closer to their Lord and thee.

[122] The Lord hath made all things for Himself: year, even the wicked for the day of evil. Proverbs xvi. 4.
[123] Philippians i. 21.
[124] In the Epistle to the Philippians, 'I know that I shall abide andcontinue with you all: - I count not myself to have apprehenede.' chaps. 1.25; iii. 13. In 2 Timothy, 'I have finished my course,' &c., ch. iv. 7, 8.
[125] The Gospel of Luke abounds most in such passages as the parable of the lost sheep, which display God's mercy to penitent sinners.
[126] The Christian hymns are all in St. Luke: the Magnificat, Benedictus,and Nunc Dimittis.

ST. SIMON AND ST. JUDE

That ye should earnestly contend for [127] the faith which was
once delivered unto the saints. St. Jude 3.

Seest thou, how tearful and alone,
And drooping like a wounded dove,
The Cross in sight, but Jesus gone,
The widow'd Church is fain to rove?

Who is at hand that loves the Lord? [128]
Make haste, and take her home, and bring
Thine household choir, in true accord
Their soothing hymns for her to sing.

Soft on her fluttering heart shall breathe
The fragrance of that genial isle,
There she may weave her funeral wreath,
And to her own sad music smile.

The Spirit of the dying Son
Is there, and fills the holy place
With records sweet of duties done,
Of pardon'd foes, and cherish'd grace.

And as of old by two and two [129]
His herald saints the Saviour sent
To soften hearts like morning dew,
Where he to shine in mercy meant;

So evermore He deems His name
Best honour'd and his way prepar'd,
When watching by his altar-flame
He sees His servants duly pair'd.

He loves when age and youth are met,
Fervent old age and youth serene,
Their high and low in concord set
For sacred song, Joy's golden mean.

He loves when some clear soaring mind
Is drawn by mutual piety
To simple souls and unrefin'd,
Who in life's shadiest covert lie.

Or if perchance a sadden'd heart
That once was gay and felt the spring,
Cons slowly o'er its alter'd part,
In sorrow and remorse to sing,

Thy gracious care will send that way
Some spirit full of glee, yet taught
To bear the sight of dull decay,
And nurse it with all-pitying thought;

Cheerful as soaring lark, and mild
As evening blackbird's dull-toned lay,
When the relenting sun has smil'd
Bright through a whole December day.

These are the tones to brace and cheer
The lonely watcher of the fold,
When nights are dark, and foeman near,
When visions fade and hearts grow cold.

How timely then a comrade's song

Comes floating on the mountain air,
And bids thee yet be bold and strong '
Fancy may die, but Faith is there.

[127] 'be very anxious for it:' 'feel for it as for a friend in jeop-
ardy.'
[128] Then saith He to the disciple, Behold thy mother! And from
that hour that disciple took her into his own home. St. John xix.
27.
[129] St. Mark vi. 7; St. Luke x. 1.

ALL SAINTS' DAY.

Hurt not the earth, neither the sea, nor the trees, till we have sealed the servants of our God in their foreheads. Revelations vii. 3.

Why blow'st thou not, thou wintry wind,
Now every leaf is brown and sere,
And idly droops, to thee resign'd,
The fading chaplet of the year?
Yet wears the pure aerial sky
Her summer veil, half drawn on high,
Of silvery haze, and dark and still
The shadows sleep on every slanting hill.

How quiet shows the woodland scene!
Each flower and tree, its duty done,
Reposing in decay serene,
Like weary men when age is won,
Such calm old age as conscience pure
And self-commanding hearts ensure,
Waiting their summons to the sky,
Content to live, but not afraid to die.

Sure if our eyes were purg'd to trace
God's unseen armies hovering round,
We should behold by angels' grace
The four strong winds of Heaven fast bound,

Their downward sweep a moment stay'd
On ocean cove and forest glade,
Till the last flower of autumn shed
Her funeral odours on her dying bed.

So in Thine awful armoury, Lord,
The lightnings of the judgment-day
Pause yet awhile, in mercy stor'd,
Till willing hearts wear quite away
Their earthly stains; and spotless shine
On every brow in light divine
The Cross by angel hands impress'd,
The seal of glory won and pledge of promis'd rest.

Little they dream, those haughty souls
Whom empires own with bended knee,
What lowly fate their own controls,
Together link'd by Heaven's decree; -
As bloodhounds hush their baying wild
To wanton with some fearless child,
So Famine waits, and War with greedy eyes,
Till some repenting heart be ready for the skies.

Think ye the spires that glow so bright
In front of yonder setting sun,
Stand by their own unshaken might?
No - where th' upholding grace is won,
We dare not ask, nor Heaven would tell,
But sure from many a hidden dell,
From many a rural nook unthought of there,
Rises for that proud world the saints' prevailing prayer.

On, Champions blest, in Jesus' name,
Short be your strife, your triumph full,
Till every heart have caught your flame,
And, lighten'd of the world's misrule,
Ye soar those elder saints to meet

THE CHRISTIAN YEAR

Gather'd long since at Jesus' feet,
No world of passions to destroy,
Your prayers and struggles o'er, your task all praise and joy.

HOLY COMMUNION

O God of mercy, God of might,
How should pale sinners bear the sight,
If, as Thy power in surely here,
Thine open glory should appear?

For now Thy people are allow'd
To scale the mount and pierce the cloud,
And Faith may feed her eager view
With wonders Sinai never knew.

Fresh from th' atoning sacrifice
The world's Creator bleeding lies.
That man, His foe, by whom He bled,
May take Him for his daily bread.

O agony of wavering thought
When sinners first so near are brought!
'It is my Maker - dare I stay?
My Saviour - dare I turn away?'

Thus while the storm is high within
'Twixt love of Christ and fear of sin,
Who can express the soothing charm,
To feel Thy kind upholding arm,

My mother Church? and hear thee tell
Of a world lost, yet loved so well,
That He, by whom the angels live,

His only Son for her would give? [130]

And doubt we yet? Thou call'st again;
A lower still, a sweeter strain;
A voice from Mercy's inmost shrine,
This very breath of Love divine.

Whispering it says to each apart,
'Come unto Me, thou trembling heart;' [131]
And we must hope, so sweet the tone,
The precious words are all our own.

Hear them, kind Saviour - hear Thy Spouse
Low at Thy feet renew her vows;
Thine own dear promise she would plead
For us her true though fallen seed.

She pleads by all Thy mercies, told
Thy chosen witnesses of old,
Love's heralds sent to man forgiven,
One from the Cross, and one from Heaven. [132]

This, of true Penitents the chief,
To the lost spirit brings relief,
Lifting on high th' adored Name: '
'Sinners to save, Christ, Jesus came.' [133]

That, dearest of Thy bosom Friends,
Into the wavering heart descends: '
'What? fallen again? yet cheerful rise. [134]
Thine Intercessor never dies.'

The eye of Faith, that waxes bright
Each moment by thine altar's light,
Sees them e'en now: they still abide
In mystery kneeling at our side:

And with them every spirit blest,
From realms of triumph or of rest,
From Him who saw creation's morn,
Of all Thine angels eldest born,

To the poor babe, who died to-day,
Take part in our thanksgiving lay,
Watching the tearful joy and calm,
While sinners taste Thine heavenly balm.

Sweet awful hour! the only sound
One gentle footstep gliding round,
Offering by turns on Jesus' part
The Cross to every hand and heart.

Refresh us, Lord, to hold it fast;
And when Thy veil is drawn at last,
Let us depart where shadows cease,
With words of blessing and of peace.

[130] 'So God loved the world, that He gave His only begotten
Son.' See the sentence in the Communion Service, after the Con-
fession.
[131] Come unto Me all that travail and are heavy laden, and I will
refresh you.
[132] St. Paul and St. John.
[133] This is a true saying, and worthy of all men to be received,
That Christ Jesus came into the world to save sinners.
[134] If any man sin, we have an Advocate with the Father, Jesus
Christ the righteous.

HOLY BAPTISM

Where is it mothers learn their love? '
In every Church a fountain springs
O'er which th' Eternal Dove
Hovers out softest wings.

What sparkles in that lucid flood
Is water, by gross mortals ey'd:
But seen by Faith, 'tis blood
Out of a dear Friend's side.

A few calm words of faith and prayer,
A few bright drops of holy dew,
Shall work a wonder there
Earth's charmers never knew.

O happy arms, where cradled lies,
And ready for the Lord's embrace,
That precious sacrifice,
The darling of His grace!

Blest eyes, that see the smiling gleam
Upon the slumbering features glow,
When the life-giving stream
Touches the tender brow!

Or when the holy cross is sign'd,
And the young soldier duly sworn,

With true and fearless mind
To serve the Virgin-born.

But happiest ye, who seal'd and blest
Back to your arms your treasure take,
With Jesus' mark impress'd
To nurse for Jesus' sake:

To whom - as if in hallow'd air
Ye knelt before some awful shrine '
His innocent gestures wear
A meaning half divine:

By whom Love's daily touch is seen
In strengthening form and freshening hue,
In the fix'd brow serene,
The deep yet eager view. '

Who taught thy pure and even breath
To come and go with such sweet grace?
Whence thy reposing Faith,
Though in our frail embrace?

O tender gem, and full of Heaven!
Not in the twilight stars on high,
Not in moist flowers at even
See we our God so nigh.

Sweet one, make haste and know Him too,
Thine own adopting Father love,
That like thine earliest dew
Thy dying sweets may prove.

CATECHISM

Oh! say not, dream not, heavenly notes
To childish ears are vain,
That the young mind at random floats,
And cannot reach the strain.

Dim or unheard, the words may fall,
And yet the heaven-taught mind
May learn the sacred air, and all
The harmony unwind.

Was not our Lord a little child,
Taught by degrees to pray,
By father dear and mother mild
Instructed day by day?

And lov'd He not of Heaven to talk
With children in His sight,
To meet them in His daily walk,
And to His arms invite?

What though around His throne of fire
The everlasting chant
Be wafted from the seraph choir
In glory jubilant?

Yet stoops He, ever pleas'd to mark
Our rude essays of love,
Faint as the pipe of wakening lark,

KEBLE

Heard by some twilight grove:

Yet is He near us, to survey
These bright and order'd files,
Like spring-flowers in their best array,
All silence and all smiles.

Save that each little voice in turn
Some glorious truth proclaims,
What sages would have died to learn,
Now taught by cottage dames.

And if some tones be false or low,
What are all prayers beneath
But cries of babes, that cannot know
Half the deep thought they breathe?

In His own words we Christ adore,
But angels, as we speak,
Higher above our meaning soar
Than we o'er children weak:

And yet His words mean more than they,
And yet He owns their praise:
Why should we think, He turns away
From infants' simple lays?

CONFIRMATION

The shadow of th' Almighty's cloud
Calm on this tents of Israel lay,
While drooping paus'd twelve banners proud,
Till He arise and lead this way.

Then to the desert breeze unroll'd,
Cheerly the waving pennons fly,
Lion or eagle - each bright fold
A lodestar to a warrior's eye.

So should Thy champions, ere this strife
By holy hands o'ershadowed kneel,
So, fearless for their charmed life,
Bear, to this end, Thy Spirit's seal.

Steady and pure as stars that beam
In middle heaven, all mist above,
Seen deepest in this frozen stream: '
Such is their high courageous love.

And soft as pure, and warm as bright,
They brood upon life's peaceful hour,
As if the Dove that guides their flight
Shook from her plumes a downy shower.

Spirit of might and sweetness too!
Now leading on the wars of God,

Now to green isles of shade and dew
Turning the waste Thy people trod;

Draw, Holy Ghost, Thy seven-fold veil
Between us and the fires of youth;
Breathe, Holy Ghost, Thy freshening gale,
Our fever'd brow in age to soothe.

And oft as sin and sorrow tire,
This hallow'd hour do Thou renew,
When beckon'd up the awful choir
By pastoral hands, toward Thee we drew;

When trembling at this sacred rail
We hid our eyes and held our breath,
Felt Thee how strong, our hearts how frail,
And long'd to own Thee to the death.

For ever on our souls be trac'd
That blessing dear, that dove-like hand,
A sheltering rock in Memory's waste,
O'er-shadowing all the weary land.

MATRIMONY

There is an awe in mortals' joy,
A deep mysterious fear
Half of the heart will still employ,
As if we drew too near
To Eden's portal, and those fires
That bicker round in wavy spires,
Forbidding, to our frail desires,
What cost us once so dear.

We cower before th' heart-searching eye
In rapture as its pain;
E'en wedded Love, till Thou be nigh,
Dares not believe her gain:
Then in the air she fearless springs,
The breath of Heaven beneath her wings,
And leaves her woodnote wild, and sings
A tun'd and measur'd strain.

Ill fare the lay, though soft as dew
And free as air it fall,
That, with Thine altar full in view,
Thy votaries would enthrall
To a foul dream, of heathen night,
Lifting her torch in Love's despite,
And scaring with base wild-fire light
The sacred nuptial hall.

Far other strains, far other fires,

Our marriage-offering grace;
Welcome, all chaste and kind desires,
With even matron pace
Approaching down this hallow'd aisle!
Where should ye seek Love's perfect smile,
But where your prayers were learned erewhile,
In her own native place?

Where, but on His benignest brow,
Who waits to bless you here?
Living, he own'd no nuptial vow,
No bower to Fancy dear:
Love's very self - for Him no need
To nurse, on earth, the heavenly seed:
Yet comfort in His eye we read
For bridal joy and fear.

'Tis He who clasps the marriage band,
And fits the spousal ring,
Then leaves ye kneeling, hand in hand,
Out of His stores to bring
His Father's dearest blessing, shed
Of old on Isaac's nuptial bed,
Now on the board before ye spread
Of our all-bounteous King.

All blessings of the breast and womb,
Of Heaven and earth beneath,
Of converse high, and sacred home,
Are yours, in life and death.
Only kneel on, nor turn away
From the pure shrine, where Christ to-day
Will store each flower, ye duteous lay,
For an eternal wreath.

VISITATION AND COMMUNION OF THE SICK

O Youth and Joy, your airy tread
Too lightly springs by Sorrow's bed,
Your keen eye-glances are too bright,
Too restless for a sick man's sight.
Farewell; for one short life we part:
I rather woo the soothing art,
Which only souls in sufferings tried
Bear to their suffering brethren's side.

Where may we learn that gentle spell?
Mother of Martyrs, thou canst tell!
Thou, who didst watch thy dying Spouse
With pierced hands and bleeding brows,
Whose tears from age to age are shed
O'er sainted sons untimely dead,
If e'er we charm a soul in pain,
Thine is the key-note of our strain.

How sweet with thee to lift the latch,
Where Faith has kept her midnight watch,
Smiling on woe: with thee to kneel,
Where fix'd, as if one prayer could heal,
She listens, till her pale eye glow
With joy, wild health can never know,
And each calm feature, ere we read,
Speaks, silently, thy glorious Creed.

Such have I seen: and while they pour'd
Their hearts in every contrite word,
How have I rather long'd to kneel
And ask of them sweet pardon's seal;
How bless'd the heavenly music brought
By thee to aid my faltering thought!
'Peace' ere we kneel, and when we cease
To pray, the farewell word is, 'Peace.'

I came again: the place was bright
'With something of celestial light' '
A simple Altar by the bed
For high Communion meetly spread,
Chalice, and plate, and snowy vest. '
We ate and drank: then calmly blest,
All mourners, one with dying breath,
We sate and talk'd of Jesus' death.

Once more I came: the silent room
Was veil'd in sadly-soothing gloom,
And ready for her last abode
The pale form like a lily show'd,
By Virgin fingers duly spread,
And priz'd for love of summer fled.
The light from those soft-smiling eyes
Had fleeted to its parent skies.

O soothe us, haunt us, night and day,
Ye gentle Spirits far away,
With whom we shar'd the cup of grace,
Then parted; ye to Christ's embrace,
We to this lonesome world again,
Yet mindful of th' unearthly strain
Practis'd with you at Eden's door,
To be sung on, where Angels soar,
With blended voices evermore.

BURIAL OF THE DEAD

And when the Lord saw her, He had compassion on her, and said
unto her, Weep not. And He came and touched the bier; and they
that bare him stood still. And He said, Young man, I say unto
thee, Arise. St. Luke vii. 13, 14.

Who says, the wan autumnal sun
Beams with too faint a smile
To light up nature's face again,
And, though the year be on this wane,
With thoughts of spring the heart beguile?

Waft him, thou soft September breeze,
And gently lay him down
Within some circling woodland wall,
Where bright leaves, reddening ere they fall,
Wave gaily o'er the waters brown.

And let some graceful arch be there
With wreathed mullions proud,
With burnish'd ivy for its screen,
And moss, that glows as fresh and green
As thought beneath an April cloud. '

Who says the widow's heart must break,
The childless mother sink? '
A kinder truer voice I hear,
Which e'en beside that mournful bier

Whence parents' eyes would hopeless shrink,

Bids weep no more - O heart bereft,
How strange, to thee, that sound!
A widow o'er her only son,
Feeling more bitterly alone
For friends that press officious round.

Yet is the voice of comfort heard,
For Christ hath touch'd the bier '
The bearers wait with wondering eye,
The swelling bosom dares not sigh,
But all is still, 'twixt hope and fear.

E'en such an awful soothing calm
We sometimes see alight
On Christian mourners, while they wait
In silence, by some churchyard gate,
Their summons to this holy rite.

And such the tones of love, which break
The stillness of that hour,
Quelling th' embitter'd spirit's strife '
'The Resurrection and the Life
Am I: believe, and die no more.'

Unchang'd that voice - and though not yet
The dead sit up and speak,
Answering its call; we gladlier rest
Our darlings on earth's quiet breast,
And our hearts feel they must not break.

Far better they should sleep awhile
Within the Church's shade,
Nor wake, until new heaven, new earth,
Meet for their new immortal birth
For their abiding-place be made,

Than wander back to life, and lean
On our frail love once more.
'Tis sweet, as year by year we lose
Friends out of sight, in faith to muse
How grows in Paradise our store.

Then pass, ye mourners, cheerly on,
Through prayer unto the tomb,
Still, as ye watch life's falling leaf,
Gathering from every loss and grief
Hope of new spring and endless home.

Then cheerly to your work again
With hearts new-brac'd and set
To run, untir'd, love's blessed race.
As meet for those, who face to face
Over the grave their Lord have met.

CHURCHING OF WOMEN

Is there, in bowers of endless spring,
One known from all the seraph band
By softer voice, by smile and wing
More exquisitely bland!
Here let him speed: to-day this hallow'd air
Is fragrant with a mother's first and fondest prayer.

Only let Heaven her fire impart,
No richer incense breathes on earth:
'A spouse with all a daughter's heart,.'
Fresh from the perilous birth,
To the great Father lifts her pale glad eye,
Like a reviving flower when storms are hush'd on high.

Oh, what a treasure of sweet thought
Is here! what hope and joy and love
All in one tender bosom brought,
For the all-gracious Dove
To brood o'er silently, and form for Heaven
Each passionate wish and dream to dear affection given.

Her fluttering heart, too keenly blest,
Would sicken, but she leans on Thee,
Sees Thee by faith on Mary's breast,
And breathes serene and free.
Slight tremblings only of her veil declare [135]
Soft answers duly whisper'd to each soothing prayer.

We are too weak, when Thou dost bless,
To bear the joy - help, Virgin-born!
By Thine own mother's first caress,
That wak'd Thy natal morn!
Help, by the unexpressive smile, that made
A Heaven on earth around this couch where Thou wast laid.

[135] When the woman comes to this office, the rubric (as it was altered at the last review) directs that she be decently apparelled, i.e., as the custom and order was formerly, with a white covering or veil. Wheatly on the Common Prayer, c. xiii. sect. i. 3.

COMMINATION

The prayers are o'er: why slumberest thou so long,
Thou voice of sacred song?
Why swell'st thou not, like breeze from mountain cave,
High o'er the echoing nave,
The white-robed priest, as otherwhile, to guide,
Up to the Altar's northern side? '
A mourner's tale of shame and sad decay
Keeps back our glorious sacrifice to-day:

The widow'd Spouse of Christ: with ashes crown'd,
Her Christmas robes unbound,
She lingers in the porch for grief and fear,
Keeping her penance drear, '
Oh, is it nought to you? that idly gay,
Or coldly proud, ye turn away?
But if her warning tears in vain be spent,
Lo, to her alter'd eye this Law's stern fires are lent.

Each awful curse, that on Mount Ebal rang,
Peals with a direr clang
Out of that silver trump, whose tones of old
Forgiveness only told.
And who can blame the mother's fond affright, [136]
Who sporting on some giddy height
Her infant sees, and springs with hurried hand
To snatch the rover from the dangerous strand?

But surer than all words the silent spell

(So Grecian legends tell)
When to her bird, too early 'scap'd the nest,
She bares her tender breast,
Smiling he turns and spreads his little wing,
There to glide home, there safely cling.
So yearns our mother o'er each truant son,
So softly falls the lay in fear and wrath begun.

Wayward and spoil'd she knows ye: the keen blast,
That brac'd her youth, is past:
The rod of discipline, the robe of shame '
She bears them in your name:
Only return and love. But ye perchance
Are deeper plung'd in sorrow's trance:
Your God forgives, but ye no comfort take
Till ye have scourg'd the sins that in your conscience ache.

Oh, heavy laden soul! kneel down and hear
Thy penance in calm fear:
With thine own lips to sentence all thy sin;
Then, by the judge within
Absolv'd, in thankful sacrifice to part
For ever with thy sullen heart,
Nor on remorseful thoughts to brood, and stain
This glory of the Cross, forgiven and cheereth in vain.

[136] Alluding to a beautiful anecdote in the Greek Anthology, tom. i. 180, ed. Jacobs. See Pleasures and Memory, p. 133.

FORMS OF PRAYER TO BE USED AT SEA

When thou passest through the waters, I will be with thee.
Isaiah xliii. 2.

The shower of moonlight falls as still and clear
Upon this desert main
As where sweet flowers some pastoral garden cheer
With fragrance after rain:
The wild winds rustle in piping shrouds,
As in the quivering trees:
Like summer fields, beneath the shadowy clouds
The yielding waters darken in the breeze.

Thou too art here with thy soft inland tones,
Mother of our new birth;
The lonely ocean learns thy orisons,
And loves thy sacred mirth:
When storms are high, or when the fires of war
Come lightening round our course,
Thou breath'st a note like music from afar,
Tempering rude hearts with calm angelic force.

Far, far away, the homesick seaman's hoard,
Thy fragrant tokens live,
Like flower-leaves in a previous volume stor'd,
To solace and relieve

Some heart too weary of the restless world;
Or like thy Sabbath Cross,
That o'er this brightening billow streams unfurl'd,
Whatever gale the labouring vessel toss.

Oh, kindly soothing in high Victory's hour,
Or when a comrade dies,
In whose sweet presence Sorrow dares not lower,
Nor Expectation rise
Too high for earth; what mother's heart could spare
To the cold cheerless deep
Her flower and hope? but Thou art with him there,
Pledge of the untir'd arm and eye that cannot sleep:

The eye that watches o'er wild Ocean's dead,
Each in his coral cave,
Fondly as if the green turf wrapt his head
Fast by his father's grave, '
One moment, and the seeds of life shall spring
Out of the waste abyss,
And happy warriors triumph with their King
In worlds without a sea, [137] unchanging orbs of bliss.

[137] And there was no more sea. Revelations xxi. 1.

GUNPOWDER TREASON

A thou hast testified of Me in Jerusalem, so must thou bear wit-
ness also at Rome. Acts xxiii. 11.

Beneath the burning eastern sky
The Cross was rais'd at morn:
The widow'd Church to weep stood by,
The world, to hate and scorn.

Now, journeying westward, evermore
We know the lonely Spouse
By the dear mark her Saviour bore
Trac'd on her patient brows.

At Rome she wears it, as of old
Upon th' accursed hill:
By monarchs clad in gems and gold,
She goes a mourner still.

She mourns that tender hearts should bend
Before a meaner shrine,
And upon Saint or Angel spend
The love that should be thine.

By day and night her sorrows fall
Where miscreant hands and rude
Have stain'd her pure ethereal pall
With many a martyr's blood.

And yearns not her parental heart,
To hear their secret sighs,
Upon whose doubting way apart
Bewildering shadows rise?

Who to her side in peace would cling,
But fear to wake, and find
What they had deem'd her genial wing
Was Error's soothing blind.

She treasures up each throbbing prayer:
Come, trembler, come and pour
Into her bosom all thy care,
For she has balm in store.

Her gentle teaching sweetly blends
With this clear light of Truth
The aerial gleam that Fancy lends
To solemn thoughts in youth. '

If thou hast lov'd, in hours of gloom,
To dream the dead are near,
And people all the lonely room
With guardian spirits dear,

Dream on the soothing dream at will:
The lurid mist is o'er,
That show'd the righteous suffering still
Upon th' eternal shore.

If with thy heart the strains accord,
That on His altar-throne
Highest exalt thy glorious Lord,
Yet leave Him most thine own;

Oh, come to our Communion Feast:

There present, in the heart
As in the hands, th' eternal Priest
Will His true self impart. '

Thus, should thy soul misgiving turn
Back to th' enchanted air,
Solace and warning thou mayst learn
From all that tempts thee there.

And, oh! by all the pangs and fears
Fraternal spirits know,
When for an elder's shame the tears
Of wakeful anguish flow,

Speak gently of our sister's fall:
Who knows but gentle love
May win her at our patient call
The surer way to prove?

KING CHARLES THE MARTYR

This is thankworthy, if a man for conscience toward God endure
grief, suffering wrongfully. 1 St. Peter ii. 19.

Praise to our pardoning God! though silent now
The thunders of the deep prophetic sky,
Though in our sight no powers of darkness bow
Before th' Apostles' glorious company;

The Martyrs' noble army still is ours,
Far in the North our fallen days have seen
How in her woe this tenderest spirit towers
For Jesus' sake in agony serene.

Praise to our God! not cottage hearths alone,
And shades impervious to the proud world's glare,
Such witness yield; a monarch from his throne
Springs to his Cross and finds his glory there.

Yes: whereso'er one trace of thee is found,
As in the Sacred Land, the shadows fall:
With beating hearts we roam the haunted ground,
Lone battle-field, or crumbling prison hall.

And there are aching solitary breasts,
Whose widow'd walk with thought of thee is cheer'd
Our own, our royal Saint: thy memory rests
On many a prayer, the more for thee endear'd.

True son of our dear Mother, early taught
With her to worship and for her to die,
Nurs'd in her aisles to more than kingly thought,
Oft in her solemn hours we dream thee nigh.

For thou didst love to trace her daily lore,
And where we look for comfort or for calm,
Over the self-same lines to bend, and pour
Thy heart with hers in some victorious psalm.

And well did she thy loyal love repay;
When all forsook, her Angels still were nigh,
Chain'd and bereft, and on thy funeral way,
Straight to the Cross she turn'd thy dying eye [138]

And yearly now, before the Martyrs' King,
For thee she offers her maternal tears,
Calls us, like thee, to His dear feet to cling,
And bury in His wounds our earthly fears.

The Angels hear, and there is mirth in Heaven,
Fit prelude of the joy, when spirits won
Like those to patient Faith, shall rise forgiven,
And at their Saviour's knees thy bright example own.

[138] 'His Majesty then bade him (Mr. Herbert) withdraw; for he was about an hour in private with the Bishop (Juxon): and being called in, the Bishop went to prayer; and reading also the 27th chapter of the Gospel of St. Matthew, which relateth the Passion of our Blessed Saviour. The King, after the Service was done, asked the Bishop, if he had made choice of that chapter, being so applicable to his present condition? The Bishop replied, 'May it please your Gracious Majesty, it is the proper lesson for the day, as appears by the Kalendar;' which the King was much affected with, so aptly serving as a seasonable preparation for his death that day.' Herbert's Memoirs, p. 131.

THE RESTORATION OF THE ROYAL FAMILY

And Barzillai said unto the King, How long have I to live, that I
should go up with the King unto Jerusalem? 2 Samuel xix. 34.

As when the Paschal week is o'er,
Sleeps in the silent aisles no more
The breath of sacred song,
But by the rising Saviour's light
Awaken'd soars in airy flight,
Or deepening rolls along; [139]

The while round altar, niche, and shrine,
The funeral evergreens entwine,
And a dark brilliance cast,
The brighter for their hues of gloom,
Tokens of Him, who through the tomb
Into high glory pass'd:

Such were the lights and such the strains.
When proudly stream'd o'er ocean plains
Our own returning Cross;
For with that triumph seem'd to float
Far on the breeze one dirge-like note
Of orphanhood and loss.

Father and King, oh where art thou?

A greener wreath adorns thy brow,
And clearer rays surround;
O, for one hour of prayer like thine,
To plead before th' all-ruling shrine
For Britain lost and found!

And he, [140] whose mild persuasive voice
Taught us in trials to rejoice,
Most like a faithful dove,
That by some ruin'd homestead builds,
And pours to the forsaken fields
His wonted lay of love:

Why comes he not to bear his part,
To lift and guide th' exulting heart? '
A hand that cannot spars
Lies heavy on his gentle breast:
We wish him health; he sighs for rest,
And Heaven accepts the prayer.

Yes, go in peace, dear placid spright,
Ill spar'd; but would we store aright
Thy serious sweet farewell,
We need not grudge thee to the skies,
Sure after thee in time to rise,
With thee for ever dwell.

Till then, whene'er with duteous hand,
Year after year, my native Land
Her royal offering brings,
Upon the Altar lays the Crown,
And spreads her robes of old renown
Before the King of kings.

Be some kind spirit, likest thine,
Ever at hand, with airs divine
The wandering heart to seize;

Whispering, 'How long hast thou to live,
That thou should'st Hope or Fancy gave
To flowers or crowns like these?'

[139] The organ is silent in many Churches during Passion week:
and in some it is the custom to put up evergreen boughs at Easter
as well as at Christmas time.
[140] Read Fell's Life of Hammond, p. 283-296. Oxford, 1806.

THE ACCESSION

As I was with Moses, so I will be with thee; I will not fail thee,
nor forsake thee. Joshua i. 5.

The voice that from the glory came
To tell how Moses died unseen,
And waken Joshua's spear of flame
To victory on the mountains green,
Its trumpet tones are sounding still,
When Kings or Parents pass away,
They greet us with a cheering thrill
Of power and comfort in decay.

Behind thus soft bright summer cloud
That makes such haste to melt and die,
Our wistful gaze is oft allow'd
A glimpse of the unchanging sky:
Let storm and darkness do their worst;
For the lost dream the heart may ache,
The heart may ache, but may not burst;
Heaven will not leave thee nor forsake.

One rock amid the weltering floods,
One torch in a tempestuous night,
One changeless pine in fading woods: '
Such is the thought of Love and Might,
True Might and ever-present Love,
When death is busy near the throne,

Auth Sorrow her keen sting would prove
On Monarchs orphan'd and alone.

In that lorn hour and desolate,
Who could endure a crown? but He,
Who singly bore the world's sad weight,
Is near, to whisper, 'Lean on Me:
Thy days of toil, thy nights of care,
Sad lonely dreams in crowded hall,
Darkness within, while pageants glare
Around - the Cross supports them all.'

Oh, Promise of undying Love!
While Monarchs seek thee for repose,
Far in the nameless mountain cove
Each pastoral heart thy bounty knows.
Ye, who in place of shepherds true
Come trembling to their awful trust,
Lo here the fountain to imbue
With strength and hope your feeble dust.

Not upon Kings or Priests alone
The power of that dear word is spent;
It chants to all in softest tone
The lowly lesson of Content:
Heaven's light is pour'd on high and low;
To high and low Heaven's Angel spake;
'Resign thee to thy weal or woe,
I ne'er will leave thee nor forsake.'

ORDINATION

After this, the congregation shall be desired, secretly in their
prayers, to make their humble supplications to God for all these
things: for the which prayers there shall be silence kept for a
space. After which shall be sung or said by the Bishop (the per-
sons to be ordained Priests all kneeling), 'Veni, Creator
Spiritus.' - Rubric in the Office for Ordering of Priests.

'Twas silence in Thy temple, Lord,
When slowly through the hallow'd air
The spreading cloud of incense soar'd,
Charg'd with the breath of Israel's prayer.

'Twas silence round Thy throne on high,
When the last wondrous seal unclos'd, [141]
And in this portals of the sky
Thine armies awfully repos'd.

And this deep pause, that o'er us now
Is hovering - comes it not of Thee?
Is it not like a mother's vow
When, with her darling on her knee,

She weighs and numbers o'er and o'er
Love's treasure hid in her fond breast,
To cull from that exhaustless store
The dearest blessing and the best?

And where shall mother's bosom find,
With all its deep love-learned skill,
A prayer so sweetly to her mind,
As, in this sacred hour and still,

Is wafted from the white-rob'd choir,
Ere yet the pure high-breathed lay,
'Come, Holy Ghost, our souls inspire,.'
Rise floating on its dove-like way.

And when it comes, so deep and clear
The strain, so soft the melting fall,
It seems not to th' entranced ear
Less than Thine own heart-cheering call.

Spirit of Christ - Thine earnest given
That these our prayers are heard, and they,
Who grasp, this hour, the sword of Heaven,
Shall feel Thee on their weary way.

Oft as at morn or soothing eve
Over the Holy Fount they lean,
Their fading garland freshly weave,
Or fan them with Thine airs serene.

Spirit of Light and Truth! to Thee
We trust them in that musing hour,
Till they, with open heart and free.
Teach all Thy word in all its power.

When foemen watch their tents by night,
And mists hang wide o'er moor and fell,
Spirit of Counsel and of Might,
Their pastoral warfare guide Thou well.

And, O! when worn and tir'd they sigh

With that more fearful war within,
When Passion's storms are loud and high,
And brooding o'er remember'd sin

The heart dies down - O, mightiest then,
Come ever true, come ever near,
And wake their slumbering love again,
Spirit of God's most holy Fear!

[141] When He had opened the seventh seal, there was silence in
Heaven about the space of half an hour. Rev. viii. 1.

You may also enjoy ...

Wandering Between Two Worlds: Essays on Faith and Art
Anita Mathias
Benediction Books, 2007
152 pages
ISBN: 0955373700

Available from www.amazon.com, www.amazon.co.uk
www.wanderingbetweentwoworlds.com

In these wide-ranging lyrical essays, Anita Mathias writes, in lush, lovely prose, of her naughty Catholic childhood in Jamshedpur, India; her large, eccentric family in Mangalore, a sea-coast town converted by the Portuguese in the sixteenth century; her rebellion and atheism as a teenager in her Himalayan boarding school, run by German missionary nuns, St. Mary's Convent, Nainital; and her abrupt religious conversion after which she entered Mother Teresa's convent in Calcutta as a novice. Later rich, elegant essays explore the dualities of her life as a writer, mother, and Christian in the United States-- Domesticity and Art, Writing and Prayer, and the experience of being "an alien and stranger" as an immigrant in America, sensing the need for roots.

About the Author

Anita Mathias was born in India, has a B.A. and M.A. in English from Somerville College, Oxford University and an M.A. in Creative Writing from the Ohio State University. Her essays have been published in The Washington Post, The London Magazine, The Virginia Quarterly Review, Commonweal, Notre Dame Magazine, America, The Christian Century, Religion Online, The Southwest Review, Contemporary Literary Criticism, New Letters, The Journal, and two of HarperSanFrancisco's The Best Spiritual Writing anthologies. Her non-fiction has won fellowships from The National Endowment for the Arts; The Minnesota State Arts Board; The Jerome Foundation, The Vermont Studio Center; The Virginia Centre for the Creative Arts, and the First Prize for the Best General Interest Article from the Catholic Press Association of the United States and Canada. Anita has taught Creative Writing at the College of William and Mary, and now lives and writes in Oxford, England.
Website: www.anitamathias.com/
Blog: wanderingbetweentwoworlds.blogspot.com/

www.ingramcontent.com/pod-product-compliance
Lightning Source LLC
Chambersburg PA
CBHW030522100426
42813CB00001B/118